Software
Testing Techniques

Joe Abbott

PUBLISHED BY NCC PUBLICATIONS

British Library Cataloguing in Publication Data

Abbott Joe
  Software testing techniques.
  1. Computer Programs — Testing
  I. Title
  005.3'0287   QA76.76.T48
  ISBN 0-85012-419-0

First published in 1986 by:

NCC Publications, The National Computing Centre Limited, Oxford Road, Manchester M1 7ED, England.

Typeset in 11pt Times Roman by Manntype Typesetting Specialists, Fourways House, 18 Tariff Street, Manchester M1 2EP; and printed by Hobbs the Printers of Southampton.

ISBN 0-85012-419-0

Acknowledgements

Much of the basic material for this book was collected in a research programme undertaken jointly by the National Computing Centre Limited and the Gesellschaft für Mathematik und Datenverarbeitung of Bonn, West Germany, during 1983 and 1984. This research programme, entitled 'The Specification and Development of Software Systems', was sponsored by the Commission of the European Communities and the National Governments of the UK and West Germany.

Thanks are due to the Commission of the European Communities and the UK Electronics and Avionics Requirements Board for jointly funding the programme.

Contents

1 Introduction

GENERAL

This book is aimed at commerce, industry and the public sector. It is concerned with quality control in the production of computer software used in business administration, and deals specifically with the evaluation and proving of the correctness of such software.

WHAT IS CORRECTNESS?

Correctness is a *key attribute* of computer software. Without correctness a system can hardly be user-friendly. Without correctness, superior performance is of no value, and efficient use is virtually impossible.

A computer system may be correct in a variety of ways. It may be correct in an abstract sense, ie the system may be in some way *inherently perfect*. It may be correct in the sense that it is a *perfect reflection of its user's expectations*. Or it may be technically or contractually correct, ie it *functions in accordance with the expressed, specified wishes of its users*.

In business, abstract correctness is of no real interest. The correctness which is sought is correctness in the eyes of the user. This is generally achieved by breaking the correctness problem into two: first, assuring that the system specification reflects the user's wishes; second, assuring that the system functions as specified. This book deals primarily with the second part of the problem: 'proving' that software functions as specified.

WHAT DO WE MEAN BY PROVING?

If the word 'proving' is used in the strict sense, it would be true to say that:
— if software is proven correct, it is correct;
— if software is not correct, it cannot be proven correct.

The implication is that proving establishes, *absolutely,* that a piece of software is correct.

Currently, as we will see, there is *no* method of establishing the correctness of software with absolute certainty — no way of *proving* software correct. Despite this, the term 'proving' is frequently used in this book to stress that testing should *seek* absolute proof. In practice, testers and industry alike must accept that all that testing can really provide is a high degree of confidence in the correctness of software.

HOW DO WE PROVE CORRECTNESS?

In days gone by, testing was seen as *the* means of proving software correct. Now it is well recognised that testing cannot stand on its own. The approach which should be adopted is the more persistent approach of life-cycle quality assurance.

In theory, quality assurance reflects the maxim 'start right, stay right'. It aims to establish the correctness of the software concept right at the beginning of development and then establish that every derivation of this concept is consistent with the original. The ultimate result of such a process must, in theory, be correct software.

In practice, we can no more prove the correctness of a software concept than we can prove the correctness of finished software. Quality assurance then might be better seen as a process of repeatedly trying to establish correctness, by eliminating incorrectness. It reflects the maxim 'if at first you don't succeed...' . If we try to establish the correctness of software hard enough, and often enough, we will ultimately produce software which is 'near enough' to correct.

THE BOOK ITSELF

The next two chapters are concerned broadly with software quality control rather than with software testing. Chapter 2 provides an overview of the complete quality assurance process, whilst Chapter 3 discusses techniques for reviewing documents – techniques at the heart of most quality assurance not based on software testing.

The purpose of these initial chapters is to make the tester aware of what is going on around him and thus to put software testing into perspective.

Subsequent chapters deal specifically with software testing. Their aim is to convey an understanding of the theory and techniques of testing, which will help testers in their day-to-day working lives.

Chapter 9 provides a glimpse of what the future may hold, and the book concludes with a restatement of the most vital points made in preceding chapters.

The aim of this book is primarily educational. It is to provide, for the competent, an awareness and understanding. In no sense can it be considered an idiot's guide to testing: software testing is not a job for idiots – it requires intellectual skill and effort. Just how much, may become evident in reading the book.

2 The Quality Assurance Life Cycle

INTRODUCTION

There was a time, in the early days of computing, when people believed that they were inherently capable of producing correct software at the first attempt. Experience soon proved them wrong.

Having recognised their ability to make mistakes, the pioneers of computing started to 'test' their finished programs before using them operationally. Initially, the pioneers saw testing as the total solution to the defect problem. But in those days, systems analysis hardly existed, design had not really been invented, users were less aware and less vocal, and the systems were simpler. As software development processes and the software itself became more complicated, and users became more competent and demanding, it became obvious that something more than mere testing was required to ensure the development of correct, quality software. What was needed was 'life-cycle quality assurance'.

In theory, the life-cycle approach to quality assurance involves getting the system right, right at the start of development, and ensuring that it stays right from then on. In practice, quality assurance is not yet so precise. But despite the imperfections of current quality-assurance methods, today it is essential that they be practised throughout system development. Development costs are high, and it makes no sense to pour such money into development, and *then* to find out that the money was wasted; development takes

13

considerable time and is often carried out against a background of pressure of time; it makes no sense to ignore problems until there is no time left to solve them.

The remainder of this chapter outlines, stage by stage, the practices of life-cycle-long quality assurance. The prime aim is to put the role and significance of software testing into perspective.

ANALYSIS AND DESIGN

The total process of analysis and design is complex: it can be broken into a number of stages in a number of ways. One approach is to subdivide the process into requirements specification and analysis, business systems design, computer system design, and program design. From a quality assurance viewpoint, how the process is broken down is not so important. What matters are the interim products of development.

The creation of interim products, usually in a documentary form, is necessary to provide an opportunity to control quality. In theory, each interim product can and should be validated for completeness, for internal consistency, for consistency with its predecessor or source, and for consistency with original requirements. Checks should be carried out as soon as possible: early checking can avoid the substantial costs associated with the misdirection of effort and remedial work.

In these early stages of development, quality assurance is essential not only for quality reasons, but also to facilitate progress control. Progress control can only be truly effective if it can be 'proven' that some particular activity has been *completed*. Quality assurance provides such proof. Quality assurance is most valuable in the early stages of development; but, inconveniently, it is also most difficult at that time.

In practice, analysis and design are often little more than informal processes, and their products are often loosely structured. Such processes and products do not provide a sufficiently firm and determinate foundation on which to build a quality assurance procedure. At present, quality assurance in analysis and design rests primarily on the practices of review (described in Chapter 3).

Quality assurance in the early stages is intellectually difficult.

A vast amount of checking and cross-checking within an often stretched timescale may also be involved. In such circumstances it is apparent that quality assurance during analysis and design is likely to be imperfect.

The hard-headed accountant might weigh the potential costs and benefits of quality assurance in the early stages of development and decide to cut the company's losses. From a testing viewpoint, such an action is undesirable. The more defective the software at the start of test, the more complex and time-consuming the necessary test process. Expediency may curtail quality assurance in the early stages of development, but the part of quality assurance devoted to establishing the correctness of software should not be sacrificed.

MODULE TESTING

The term 'module testing' is used here to encompass all procedures involving the testing of parts of a program in isolation. It is the first phase of testing and is regarded by many as a preliminary to 'real' testing.

The phase of module testing is, more so than other phases of testing, potentially dual-purpose. Module testing involves the testing of new untried code which can be presumed to include some faults and errors. It must seek to bring these faults to light so that they can be removed. In addition, module testing should represent the first part of an exercise in 'proving' or 'measuring' correctness.

The dual purpose of module testing is a problem. Proving and measurement are deliberate processes concentrating on the overall picture. Fault-finding, on the other hand, particularly interactive fault-finding, is a dynamic activity mainly concerned with details. Fault-finding is a necessity and, it must be admitted, is often more attractive to programmers. Consequently, in practice, the aims of measurement and proving can get lost. It is when and because these aims do get lost that module testing becomes a preliminary to 'real' testing: module testing becomes merely a debugging exercise.

Logically, the aims of fault-finding and evaluation are not really in conflict. Both can, and should, make use of the same comprehensive test set. Processing of this test set in its entirety without error indicates the end of module testing and implies that the module is as correct as the test set is comprehensive. Before this happens however, errors will likely be brought to light and quite possibly additional test sets will be improvised in order to characterise or to locate faults. Such additional tests are of no importance in evaluation and can (and really should) be forgotten when they have served their purpose.

If module testing is to play an effective part in the evaluation of correctness, it is important to pay attention to discipline and control.

A comprehensive test set cannot be developed prior to module testing, so it is necessary to keep records of the test set as it grows. The problem of improvised tests must also be dealt with. Unless the test set is documented and controlled, it is easy to end up in a situation where it is uncertain what the module *should* be tested with.

Whilst errors are being detected, it is quite likely that only a part of the test set will be run at any one time and, moreover, the module under test will be continually changing. Without good effective control, it is easy to lose track of what a module *has* been tested with.

The module testing process is obviously at its simplest and most efficient when testing error-free code. The more errors slip through earlier quality assurance, the more inefficient and confused the process becomes, the more cash is poured down the drain and the less confidence can be placed in the testing process. Some might of course say that testing error-free code is a waste of time and effort. It is not. It provides what businessmen consider to be a precious commodity − assurance − assurance that the software actually works.

INTEGRATION TESTING

The phase of integration testing is an intermediate phase between module testing and system testing. It involves the testing of modules in executable combination.

In some cases, integration testing will be a single step process involving testing the system in its entirety. More often than not, however, integration testing is an iterative process involving the testing of sub-assemblies which are repeatedly integrated into larger sub-assemblies culminating in the testing of the system as a whole.

A significant practical problem in integration testing is that of planning the integration process.

Some executable combinations of modules are easy to recognise.

For example, in a batch processing system *programs* are executable *parts* of the system. Similarly, in an on-line system there may be collections of modules which constitute a transaction or transactions which are obviously chained together.

In large systems, however, simply testing at the level of programs and transactions may not be adequate. It may be necessary, or at least desirable, from a quality assurance viewpoint, to test collections of modules which constitute parts of a program or transaction. Generally, such sub-assemblies have to be identified by informal means.

Regardless of how the integration process is organised there must be some purposeful testing of the integration of modules. There are two aspects to consider:

–   the testing of interfaces between modules;

–   the testing of the interface between the integrated assembly and its environment.

Ensuring Internal Consistency

The problem of ensuring that modules interface correctly can itself be broken into two components: physical and logical interfacing. Physical interfacing is concerned with the structure and form of the interfaces. Logical interfacing is concerned with the semantic content of the interfaces. These terms are best explained by example.

At the physical level, a module may invoke another module and pass across a number of records. It must be verified in some way that both modules assume that the same records are passed across, that where necessary these records are presented in the same order, that they include identical elements of data and that the elements of data are in the same order. At the logical level, it must be proven that if the called module assumes that a particular data item must be in the range 1 to 7, the calling module provides something in the range 1 to 7.

Proving physical consistency is something which can be done, and can probably best be done, without testing integrated software assemblies. A simple inspection of the code of interfacing modules is normally adequate.

Logical interfacing can also be demonstrated without testing integrated software assemblies. If during module testing, assertions are made concerning the values of data items passed between modules, and the modules are shown to produce and use these values, the logical compatibility of modules should not be in doubt.

If the remainder of the quality assurance process is adequate, the consistency of modules should, in integration testing, be a foregone conclusion. Integration testing should however remove reasonable remaining doubt.

Ensuring Consistency with the Environment

The aim of ensuring that the software is consistent with its environment rests on recognising that, as the software grows, new elements of code are brought into play and must be tested: file and database handling operations, for example, will not be tested when module testing with the aid of a test harness, and consequently must be tested during integration.

It is in this area that most of the value of integration testing should rest.

SYSTEM TESTING

Simplistically, system testing is the phase of testing aimed at testing the system as a whole. In practice, it is a complex activity, with numerous aims, often subdivided into a number of sequential and sometimes parallel activities.

Initially, system testing is concerned with proving that the system works correctly as a whole: ie it is merely a higher level of integration testing. Once this has been demonstrated to developers to their own satisfaction however, the process broadens in a number of dimensions. Firstly, attention is paid to attributes other than correctness, notably performance. Secondly, the business system in which the computer system is only a part becomes the object of test. Thirdly, the aim of testing moves beyond merely demonstrating technical correctness and seeks to demonstrate correctness in the eyes of users.

System testing includes many activities which go beyond the scope of this book: little will therefore be said of it. There are however points worthy of making.

System testing is the final phase of development to be followed immediately by implementation of the system: it is not therefore the time to be finding faults. Should faults appear in any number, the quality assurance and control system in use must be considered at fault. If quality assurance and control has done its job, system testing should be 'a formality': an experiment whose outcome is a foregone conclusion.

A significant feature of system testing must be the involvement of a broad range of 'users': true users, their managers, system support staff, computer operations staff and auditors. The involvement of such people introduces new problems in testing mainly resulting from the different backgrounds of the people involved. For example, users may be unable to understand the logical basis of test procedures and demand that their own (possibly over-elaborate and weak) test sets be used. They may prove to be uninterested or overdemanding. They may have changed their minds.

Many of the problems of system testing are not technical problems, but problems of communication and human nature. System testing is not the time to come to terms with such problems: they must have been dealt with continuously throughout design and development. If not, system testing is likely to be not the finale of development but the opening of hostilities between the developers and the rest of the world.

3 Reviewing Documents

INTRODUCTION

Strictly speaking, review procedures are irrelevant to correctness proving because it requires consideration of far too many details: review techniques can therefore play only a very minor role.

Review procedures are however extremely useful as a means of eliminating faults and errors which confuse the use of correctness proving techniques such as testing, static analysis and verification.

In this context, review techniques are currently extremely important. Until a software entity exists, quality control must rely on the use of review techniques of some sort: they are therefore the main means of quality control throughout the early stages of the software development life cycle.

TYPES OF REVIEW

Ad Hoc Review

In the past, ad hoc review was widely practised. In essence, it involves giving someone a document and saying "tell me what you think of that" or "what's wrong with this document?". The problem with such a review, if it can be called that, is that the reviewer is supplied with no obvious starting point, no plan of attack, no obvious end and indeed, he or she may not even understand clearly what the object of challenge is. Such a review is likely to be unreliable and irreproducible: hardly what is required for quality control purposes.

Structured Walkthroughs

A structured walkthrough is one type of 'formal' review involving 'a number of' reviewers. It is generally considered applicable to low-level designs and program code. In practice, the degree of formality varies widely as does the number of reviewers. The *scope* of walkthroughs may also vary: in some organisations, walkthroughs are concerned only with the 'correctness' of the design or code. In others, broader issues such as quality, adherence to standards, and maintainability are considered.

Prior to the walkthrough proper, the review team is supplied with copies of the document to be reviewed and any necessary supporting documentation so that they may familiarise themselves. Then at a prearranged time and place, a formal 'walkthrough' meeting is convened. At this meeting, the originator of the design or code 'walks through' it, demonstrating how it will proceed and operate on certain types of data.

The originator's purpose is to demonstrate the 'operation of' the whole design or code. Reviewers will interrupt either to ask for clarification or to note flaws in the design or code: their comments will be noted for subsequent action, but no attempt will be made to solve problems during a walkthrough.

It is generally recognised that walkthroughs should be brief: never longer than two hours; something less than an hour being the ideal.

The basic approach to walkthrough team organisation is to define a number of roles to be carried out by those involved in the walkthrough and map these roles onto real people. More than one role may be allocated to one person, but in allocating roles, care must be taken to ensure that all the roles played by one person are compatible.

Any number of 'critic' roles may be defined. Typically one reviewer will look for logical faults: another might look at the design or code with maintenance in mind, and a third might look at its general quality.

In addition to the 'critic' roles, there are administrative roles. The 'coordinator' ensures that documentation is supplied on time, before the walkthrough, and ensures that any follow up activity resulting from the walkthrough is carried out. The 'moderator' controls the walkthrough proper and the 'scribe' documents the faults recognised.

At the end of a walkthrough, the team must decide whether another walkthrough is required. It is generally recommended that a design or coded program should be walked through only once or twice. A third walkthrough tends not to be cost effective.

Inspection

The term 'inspection' is often used loosely to mean simply a visual scrutiny. In 1976, however, when Michael E Fagan, then of IBM, wrote about inspection (28), he gave the term a stricter meaning.

Inspection, in the Fagan sense, is not merely a visual scrutiny: it is a visual scrutiny with three special attributes which set it apart from other review processes. These are:

— it is a highly-directed process;

— it is 'maintained' by the use of feedback;

— it is highly formalised.

In theory, any document can be inspected: that is, a Fagan-type inspection can be created for any document. Generally however, only low-level design documentation, code and test plans are reviewed in this way. The explanation of this is two-fold. Firstly, Fagan's paper on inspection concentrates on the inspection of such documents. Secondly, documents produced at earlier stages of development are widely believed to be *less* amenable to the detailed and specific investigation characteristic of inspection.

Fagan, in his original article, presented some statistics concerning inspections. When used in evaluating system software designs and code, a 23% overall increase in productivity resulted. When an IBM user tried the same techniques on commercial work, 82% of errors were detected. Fagan's statistics suggest that the use of inspection techniques is desirable and cost effective.

Normally, prior to the inspection proper, a preparatory meeting is held to provide necessary background to the inspection team. In the case of design or code inspection, this preparatory stage is as follows.

The 'designer' describes to the inspection team, first, the overall area being addressed and then, in detail, the specific area he has designed. Documentation of the design or code is distributed. The inspection team breaks up and each individual considers the documentation primarily seeking not to find fault but to understand how the eventual software is supposed to work.

Having had time to assimilate all the background material the team reconvenes and a 'reader' proceeds to systematically step through the design or code. The process stops temporarily whenever an error is recognised. The error is clearly defined by the team as a whole and is recorded by the moderator.

Within one day of the inspection, the moderator produces a written report of the inspection and its findings.

Like walkthroughs, inspections are normally time-limited. Generally two hours is considered adequate − not because it is always possible to inspect a program in two hours but because after two hours, the senses may be dulled.

Inspection may appear to be much the same as a structured walkthrough. It is not.

A key difference between a walkthrough and an inspection revolves around 'the reader'. In a walkthrough, the producer of the document, in seeking to demonstrate the operation of the software represented by the document, will invariably *interpret* to some extent and *influence* other reviewers. In an inspection, the reader attempts to paraphrase the document, no more and no less.

Many experts believe the actions of the reader to be critical and argue that 'professional' readers should be used. In part this recommendation recognises the need for skill in readers, and in part, it aims to reduce possible bias by removing the producer of the review document from a crucial role.

In any review process, there is always a problem of 'wandering'. People involved in such processes sometimes get side-tracked. In inspection such wandering is avoided by *the use of checklists* which remind reviewers of the types of 'error' likely to occur.

This, on the one hand, makes up for deficient memories and ensures that the process is (in a sense) complete; and on the other, constrains reviewers from looking for all manner of once-in-a-lifetime problems.

Also, the inspection process must be *maintained*. As developers are faulted for making a common mistake, they start to take more care concerning that type of mistake and seek consciously to avoid making it. Eventually, they learn to avoid it without thought and it ceases to occur. As this learning process proceeds, the inspection process gradually becomes out-of-date and less cost effective. It is an essential characteristic of inspection that this *process of decay is monitored* and that when a fault ceases to occur with sufficient frequency, the search for it is discontinued.

Round Robin

A round robin review involves a meeting at which some material is presented and at which each reviewer in turn is given his or her chance to comment. It constrains comment to the end of the presentation of the material or to certain 'break' points, but ensures that all views are aired.

A potential problem is that too much material might be presented before comment is allowed. This can lead to considerable volumes of diverse comment making interaction difficult because of the lack of a focal point or the multiplicity of possible focal points.

The presentation of masses of material before comment also makes interaction between reviewers difficult because by the time discussion is allowed detailed memory of early material has failed.

The round robin is therefore appropriate to the review of 'bitty' material, for example, user documentation. The round robin is also well suited to the review of documents and aspects of documents where 'opinion' (and therefore interaction) is important.

ASPECTS OF REVIEW PROCEDURE

Introduction

In computing, procedures often come into existence and develop spontaneously and without control. Where review procedures are concerned, this must not be allowed to happen: the actual procedure of review is significant and to a considerable extent determines the thoroughness and reliability of review.

This section discusses a number of important aspects of review procedure.

Defining the Review

The key to a successful review is to ensure that reviewers understand clearly *what* is to be reviewed and *how* it is to be reviewed. This is what is meant by 'defining the review'.

The first thing to consider is what is, or are, being challenged.

Generally, the *apparent* object of review is a document: a report, specification or plan. In practice, the document as a document is normally last on the list of priorities in review. More important is some logical entity described in the document: a design, a procedure, a strategy, a program, a system, etc.

There are no simple rules for identifying the real object or objects of review. These must be identified through abstraction. In effect, all that is necessary is to identify or deduce a description of some logical entity which adequately and correctly focuses attention.

Having identified the object or objects of review, it is necessary to consider what properties or attributes of that object are of concern.

When the review procedure actually takes place, each reviewer must have only a small number of factors to consider − because the part of human memory used is extremely limited in capacity. The psychologist George A Miller suggested many years ago (in 1956) that people can temporarily remember only seven things at once. The factors each person must consider should ideally be related to some common theme. And of course, the factors to consider must, in total, be those which it is most valuable to consider. Both problems must be considered in designing a review.

Choosing the Right Time for Review

If a review is carried out too late, valuable time may be lost in correcting errors, and considerable effort may be wasted in building on the wrong foundations. On the other hand, if the review is carried out too early, the effort of review may be wasted because the product under review is changed beyond recognition following the review.

There is an optimum time for review — which is, broadly speaking, the earliest moment at which change to the product has become of minor significance. Recognising this point in time requires considerable skill, experience and considerable knowledge of the product and its impending development. It is therefore something which can only really be done by the producer of the product under review.

Having said this, it is highly desirable to exercise some measure of independent control over producers. Some are optimists and will request review at too early a stage. Some are pessimists (or perfectionists) and will leave review too late. How such independent control is implemented is a matter for individual organisations to decide.

The Size of a Review Team

It is a fact of life that the more a person has to look for, the more likely he or she is to miss something. It is for this reason that any reviewer should be given only a small number of things to look for: seven has been suggested as an appropriate number in the preceding section. If this is accepted, it follows that the total number of 'things to be looked for' determines the size of a review team. This is true, but only up to a point.

For psychological reasons, small review teams are undesirable. Everyone involved sees a conflict between the size of the group and the formality of the process. Reviewers tend to become self-conscious, and distracted, or the formality, and the concentration it demands, lapses. In either case, the rigour of review is likely to deteriorate.

Large review teams are also undesirable. If, say, twelve reviewers were to consider twelve aspects of a product in parallel at the meeting, the flow of the meeting might well be frequently broken whilst some 'fault' is outlined or some point of clarification is sought. Were this to happen, progress may be painfully slow, the motivation of reviewers would suffer, and the concentration of reviewers would likely deteriorate. Once again, the rigour of review would be comparatively low.

In view of what has been said, it is suggested that the ideal size for a review team is four to seven members. Beyond these limits, the team format becomes a negative rather than positive factor.

Management Participation

People generally believe that their working futures will be determined by their managers. Involving managers in reviews will often therefore have undesirable consequences because reviewers will seek to present the 'right' image to the managers present. In doing this, they may deliberately overlook faults in order to protect the reputation of the producer of the work under review or they may on the other hand become aggressive in order to enhance their own image. In either case, they will lose some concentration. The overall effect of management participation in reviews will often be a deterioration in review performance.

In view of the potential problems, management participation should be considered carefully. Normally, the presence of management observers should not be allowed. And management should only *contribute* to or participate in review where *necessary*.

The problems of management participation are neither universal nor insoluble. Managers who closely and continuously supervise review staff can generally participate without problem simply because it is accepted that their opinions of staff will for the most part be formed outside the review process. Other managers can in time generally become accepted if, in some direct way, it is made clear to reviewers that image building in reviews does not enhance their images.

The Involvement of Producers

Ideally, the person whose work is being reviewed should take as little part in review proceedings as possible. As any dp practitioner knows, it is quite possible for concepts to become firmly embedded in one's mind and to become accepted as fact, and as correct, even when they are fictions, or are wrong. The greater the role of the producer in a review, the more likely it is that he or she will pass on mistaken preconceptions to reviewers. It is for this reason that the use of specially trained presenters (such as code-readers) is worthy of consideration: it is not always, however, a complete solution.

It may be necessary to support the review document with background material whilst reviewers prepare themselves for the review meeting proper. Some such background material may be produced by the producer of the review document and so provides an opportunity for the producer to bias proceedings. It is therefore important to check such material before issuing it: to the extent possible, it should concentrate on fact not opinion and deal with 'what' not 'why'. In addition, reviewers should try to recognise and challenge any assumption underlying any material to be reviewed.

The Use of Aide-Memoires

It is often suggested that 'checklists' should be used in reviews. These make up for deficient memories and ensure that the review process is complete and reasonably consistent in performance. It must be noted however that during a review, a checklist *must* be virtually useless: during a review, a reviewer must be able to remember the faults he is looking for − or he will be forced to look for all faults, which will result in some loss of effectiveness. Checklists and briefing notes must therefore be seen as a means of preparing for the review rather than as an aid to be used in the review procedure itself.

Ideally, what should happen is that immediately before the review takes place, each reviewer should read any 'briefing notes' provided, thoroughly and repeatedly, until he has fixed in his mind a clear and adequately detailed definition of his role in the review.

4 The Essentials of Correctness Testing

INTRODUCTION

Software testing is the most obvious means of proving software correct — by executing the software and verifying the results produced. It is based on the assumption that:

if software cannot be shown to be incorrect, it must be correct.

It is tempting to believe that any principle so obvious must be easy to put into practice. Where testing is concerned, this is not the case.

This brief chapter outlines some of the fundamental problems which the tester must recognise and deal with.

THE BOTTOM LINE

Any program might suffer from any defect of any nature. It is impracticable to test for an infinite diversity of defects. Testing therefore can never provide conclusive proof of correctness.

It is not practicable to test software by inputting all conceivable combinations of data. Any assessment of correctness must therefore be based, to some extent, on reasoning. However, human beings are fallible, so the tester can never be absolutely sure of his reasoning. Also, in reasoning about a program, the tester must make assumptions about the operation of the program. His reasoning can only be perfect if his understanding of the program is perfect. However, given that a program might be defective in an infinite number of ways, a tester can *never* guarantee his perception, his understanding, of how a program works. It follows that, for these reasons also, testing can never provide conclusive proof of correctness.

BASIC ASSUMPTIONS

Having seen a program process one set of data and produce correct results, the novice will sometimes assume that the program is capable of repeatedly processing this, and similar data, correctly. Unwittingly, the novice has made two assumptions:

 — the program has achieved correct results by the correct method;

 — the program is consistent in its behaviour.

These assumptions are not always well-founded.

One fundamental problem in software testing is 'coincidental correctness'. A standard example of this involves the use of the value two to prove that a program can add a number to itself. Were such a program to be miscoded to multiply a number by itself, the value two would still, by coincidence, produce a correct result. In this case, the assumption that the results were achieved by the correct method would be ill-founded.

A tester could be similarly misled in testing the following programs:

 — a program which consistently references the wrong one of two data items, the two data items being generally, but not always, identical;

 — a program which references data relative to a memory address passed in a register from some other routine, the passing routine not always setting the register correctly;

 — a program which references data using absolute memory addresses, the program not always being loaded in the same area of memory.

In any of the above circumstances, the assumption that the program operated consistently would be ill-founded.

The purpose of the above text is not to attract attention (to specific checks a tester should make), but to make a general point. Any conclusions, concerning the correctness of software, drawn from testing, must rest on the assumptions that:

- coincidental correctness has not occurred during test;
- the program is consistent in its operation.

It is in practice impossible to prove these assumptions to be valid. Having recognised their existence however, a tester should consider and seek to eliminate the most obvious reasons to doubt their validity.

DETECTING DEFECTS

Essentially, software defects are of two kinds − those which can be revealed by indiscriminate execution and those which can only be revealed by executing with some critical data value or combination of data values.

Indiscriminate defects can be brought to light by simply executing the appropriate piece of code. To ensure that all such defects are brought to light, it is necessary to ensure that the software is completely executed.

The more selective defects however need to be brought to light by testing selectively − with data likely to reveal the defect. Arguably, the range of selective defects is infinite and consequently it is impossible to search for them all. What the tester must do is select and search for only the most common defects.

In practice, the most common defects are now reasonably well established and, over the years, experts have identified techniques for bringing them to light. It is primarily these techniques which are illustrated in subsequent chapters.

WHAT IS A DEFECT?

Throughout the preceding paragraphs, the term 'defect' has been used freely and without definition. Everyone assumes that they know what a defect is − a little thought however suggests they may be wrong to be so sure of themselves.

The aim of testing is sometimes stated as 'to prove that software functions as specified'. Given such a view, a defect is quite clearly and obviously a difference between what is necessary to meet the specification and what is actually coded.

This is an inadequate view.

The British Standard on software testing (2) defines correctness in the following manner:

> a system is correct if it does what it is supposed to do and does not do what it is not supposed to do.

Such a definition brings to light a pragmatic problem. Software specifications are invariably problem-oriented and concentrate on what the system *should* do: what the system should not do is at best incompletely and vaguely specified. This is why the definition of a defect as 'a divergence from the specification' is inadequate: a considerable part of the critical behaviour of the software is simply not specified. Recognition of this fact adds weight to the argument that testers must aim in part to execute software thoroughly and extends the definition of a defect to include coding which will result in *unacceptable* behaviour.

Acceptability is two-dimensional: it involves questions of whether the software 'does its job' and whether it does it in a manner satisfactorily pleasing to software users. During correctness testing, attention must be focused purely on whether the software does its job. At this point, unacceptable behaviour is purely behaviour which puts into question its ability; eg under certain conditions, the software aborts, produces misleading or stupid results, or goes into an infinite loop. The question of whether users will like what the software does must be set aside until system testing.

To set aside the question of whether users will like the software is fine in theory, but in practice, no tester can, or should, close his mind so completely. What must in practice happen is that testers remain alert to broad problems of user-acceptability, but do not 'go looking for trouble'.

5 Current Test Methods in Outline

THE AD HOC APPROACH

In the literature of testing, there is mention of a method of testing known as 'ad hoc' testing. Reading between the lines of comparative studies, it appears that experts equate ad hoc testing with 'traditional methods'.

It is clear from comparative studies that ad hoc testing is a bad method of testing — a method to be avoided. Unfortunately, no-one has ever defined ad hoc testing in terms of practices — so no organisation can tell if they are practising it.

What is assumed to make the traditional or ad hoc approach to testing inferior is the fact that it lacks any provable intellectual basis and is often practised in an ill-disciplined manner. However, the scorn which experts pour on ad hoc testing needs to be kept in perspective. Often, the roots of scientific approaches are evident in traditional environments. And discipline can be present or absent in any organisation. Cynics might accuse the experts of rigging the evidence to prove a point.

The real problem with the traditional, ad hoc method of testing is not that it can *never* work adequately but that, because the method is ill-defined, its application cannot be *guaranteed* in any way. Consequently, its adequacy can only be judged by results.

Any organisation with a real commitment to quality assurance cannot tolerate the vagueness and consequent uncertainty of the traditional ad hoc approach to software testing and, in the interests of both reliability and economy, must pursue more disciplined and defined approaches.

FUNCTIONAL TESTING

All software testing is based on the principle of feeding software with data it is required to process and verifying that the results produced are as required. What varies from method to method is primarily how, and with what purpose, test cases are generated.

In functional testing, test cases are derived through analysis of the software specification. Functional testing is essentially the traditional approach to testing practiced in a disciplined and systematic manner. At the present time however, its practice is not without problems. For functional testing to be practised, someone, at some time, must decide what constitutes a function. This requires some thought.

Most computer systems can be thought of at a variety of levels of abstraction. Therefore when looking for functions to test, testers see minor functions within major functions within even bigger functions, etc.

The tester is faced with the problem of deciding at what level of abstraction to test. If he tests at a high level of abstraction, details may be overlooked. If he tests at a low level of abstraction, he may lose sight of interactions and interdependencies between functions. What the tester needs to do is to consider the specification at various levels of abstraction.

If a tester tries to do this with a disorganised specification, he will become hopelessly confused.

A second problem of functional testing is that of 'function generation'.

The process of system development starts with a concept of a set of business functions to be computerised and proceeds to a set of coded programs by a series of transformations. Each transformation must produce something which achieves the same ends as that which preceded it, but what results from a transformation will not be *the same* as that which preceded it.

What starts as information becomes data on forms, then records on files. As these transformations occur, functions may be *generated* – first form-filling functions, then input-output functions. Once a computer system starts to take shape, security may be considered and password functions, archive and recovery functions, and error handling functions may be generated.

If the software specification is written at a high level of abstraction, it will not mention many technical functions such as file handling, error handling, etc. If test cases are derived from such a specification, testing is bound to be incomplete and inadequate. If on the other hand, the specification is written at a low level of abstraction, in order to include all the technical trivia, the user will find it difficult to understand and will not be able to verify that the specification reflects his requirements.

To suggest that there should be two specifications, one for the user and one for the tester is not really a solution because it introduces a new problem – that of ensuring the two specifications to be consistent.

From say 1973 to 1980, functional testing was largely ignored by academics in the belief that it was incapable of leading to thorough and complete testing. In 1980, however, W E (Bill) Howden of Victoria University (Canada) and the University of California (US) resurrected functional testing.

In 1980, Howden produced a paper 'Life-Cycle Software Validation' (50 or 54). In this paper, Howden implies rather than states some of his views on functional testing. It appears that Howden believes that whilst academia was concentrating on structure testing, the world of computing changed. Formal design procedures have now been developed which bring order to the whole cycle of transformations which constitute system development. Possibly, Howden suggests, in this more ordered environment, functional testing could be made to work; if not on its own, then in combination with other test methods and ideas.

Strategically speaking, it is important to develop a reliable and effective functional test approach because, firstly, functional testing can address errors of omission whereas most other test approaches cannot, and secondly, because bought-in software, parameterised packages and some 'generated' software cannot really be tested by other means.

STRUCTURE TESTING METHODS

Ad hoc and functional testing are black (or closed) box test approaches. They are pursued on the basis that nothing is known of the software under test: it is a black or closed box.

In white box (or open box) testing, the software itself is assumed to be a fountain of knowledge to be used intelligently. Exploring the use of such knowledge has suggested a number of different approaches to the test problem, the most widely known of which are the structure testing methods.

In structure testing, the source code of software is generally processed by software which inserts 'probes' at strategic points in the flow of control of the software to be tested (55). When the software is tested, execution of the probe causes some form of entry to be made in a file or database. Following a test, the 'execution history' can be analysed. Lists of the segments of code exercised and not exercised and statistical measures of 'coverage' can be produced.

The aim of structure testing is always to test 'the whole' of a program, but, as shown in Chapter 7, various approaches to structure testing adopt various views of what constitutes testing the whole of a program. The basic principle however remains constant: it is to continually measure in some way the extent to which test data has exercised program code, and to aim for some target level of execution.

PUTTING THEORY INTO PRACTICE

Neither functional testing nor structure testing is adequate when used alone.

Functional testing, because it is blind to the software under test, cannot recognise code which is surplus to requirements (eg logic bombs). Structure testing, because it is blind to the specification, cannot recognise omission.

If correctness is characterised as 'the capacity of software to do *all that it should* and *nothing it should not*', it follows that a combination of functional testing and structure testing is necessary.

Essentially, the tester must:

- develop an initial test set through some form of functional analysis;

- then use structure testing techniques to recognise gaps in the test set;

- repeatedly improve the test set until an adequate level of thoroughness has been achieved.

The next three chapters of this book support such an approach. Chapter 6 deals with the development of an initial test set, Chapter 7 with the use of structure testing, and Chapter 8 addresses the problem of measuring test thoroughness.

6 Test Sets: Problems, Construction and Use

A FUNCTIONAL APPROACH TO TEST SET CONSTRUCTION

The most common approach to the construction of test sets involves establishing the functions to be carried out by a piece of software and the test data necessary to establish that each function functions as it should.

The identification of test cases by this method is characteristic of functional testing. The problems inherent need to be recognised and dealt with if this method of test set construction is to be of any real value.

The basic problem is 'what is a function?'.

Structured programming has taught us to think of programs in terms of levels of abstraction. At one level of abstraction, a payroll system might include two elements in sequence: the first calculating gross pay; the second calculating net pay. At another level of abstraction, the net pay calculation is seen as a sequence of elements calculating tax, contributions to a pension fund, etc.

In such a system, are the higher-level, larger elements functions, or are the lower-level, smaller elements functions? Are both functions? If elements at both levels *are* functions, should both be tested? If not, how do you decide which to test?

Experience provides some guidance in answering these questions.

Typically, this approach results in up to 40% of code statements not being tested. To overcome this problem, it seems sensible to concentrate attention at the lowest level of detail possible and to aim to test the lowest-level functions rather than the high-level functions. Whether higher levels need to be tested is questionable.

Sometimes, natural language is used in specifications to describe processing. In such a specification, relationships between functions can be unclear: in part, this is because the structuring mechanisms applicable to text (sections, paragraphs, lists, etc) are not designed to show complex structures of considerable depth: in part, it is because natural language tends to include considerable 'padding'.

It is quite possible for a specification to contain a description of a high-level function and a detailed description of a low-level function comprising *one* part of the high-level function. To test thoroughly, it is necessary to test the low-level function and the part of the high-level function not otherwise specified.

Assuming that the lowest level of function always needs to be tested, one way of 'checking' the process of functional analysis is by considering what code will be associated with a function. Where a function processes data in different ways, ie using different pieces of code, the function should be considered to be a combination of functions.

If this checking process is continued to its logical conclusion, it should theoretically result in the identification of primitive functions each of which corresponds to a number of indivisible blocks of code or 'path segments'.

This implies that functional analysis can produce a test set capable of achieving the same thoroughness of testing achieved by structure testing. In practice, this is unlikely.

Specifications tend to reflect the system needed for business purposes and concentrate on business-related processing. Consequently, there may be little reference in a specification to 'technical' functions, eg checking the files used, recovery procedures, disk error handling, etc.

One way of circumventing this problem is through the use of 'error guessing'.

Experience and careful thought can in time identify the technical functions which tend to be overlooked in specifications and in the identification of test requirements. These can be listed in an aide-memoire.

Testers can then select from this list the technical test requirements they believe appropriate to any piece of software.

Such a process, because it demands decision making, is obviously potentially unreliable. However, most testers, given a list of options, should be able to decide, with reasonable reliability, what additional tests are required — and even if they miss something, an aide-memoire will invariably cause them to test more than they would otherwise do.

The process of identifying functions essentially identifies the test requirement: the requirement to prove that a function processes a given range of data. Having established the necessary range of data, it is a relatively simple task to decide values of data items representative of this range of data and thus to construct test data. The following section deals with this aspect of test case construction.

In practice, the effectiveness of this functional approach to test-data construction is heavily influenced by the manner in which software is specified.

To identify detailed test requirements it is necessary to have a clear and complete specification of each function. Sometimes however, functions are not completely specified in one place. For example, a function's processing may be outlined in one part of a specification, the data to be processed by the function may be described in another, and checking for and dealing with 'errors' in yet another part. Also, the relationships between functions, the software structure, may be unclear.

The 'disorganisation' of specifications does not make the creation of a functional test set impossible, but it certainly makes it more difficult and makes oversight more likely.

One way of improving the function-based identification of test requirements is to improve specifications in terms of both completeness and organisation. This is a topic really beyond the scope of this book.However, there are a few simple guidelines which can be of some value:

- to the extent possible, avoid the use of text in specifications;
- avoid repetition because it confuses;
- to the extent possible, structure the description of processing;
- cross-reference between sections of the specification where it is helpful;
- make use of 'standards' as aide-memoires to assure the completeness of specifications;
- be consistent in the preparation of specifications. Finding information in a number of sections is difficult, but it will be made more difficult if information is sometimes in one place, sometimes in another.

A more radical solution involves the use of highly structured specifications similar to those which result from program design. Formal specification methods such as HIPO charts may provide a means of doing this at an early rather than later stage. Ideally, however, the specification used as the basis of test should be *the* specification of the system: the specification accepted by the user. Finding a form for such a specification which is both acceptable to users and is sufficiently structured and complete for both program development and testing purposes is not easy.

In Italy, Honeywell have tried a different approach to the problem. It involves a software package TESTDOC. Essentially, TESTDOC is a word processor with special capabilities. Initially, Honeywell produce a conventional functional specification using TESTDOC as a word processor.

Subsequently, they scan the text, again using TESTDOC, and highlight phrases which could be taken to indicate functions or test requirements. As these are highlighted, they can be 'indexed'. Highlighting provides the means of stripping out the 'noise' normally present in natural language. The 'indexing' provides the means of organising the remaining text in a hierarchical form. Having carried out these operations, TESTDOC can produce what is effectively a shorthand, hopefully clearer and better-organised functional or test specification. For further details of this approach and its application see reference 20.

The techniques suggested can and generally do improve the completeness of a functional test set. They cannot, however, lead to the creation of a complete test set and cannot be guaranteed to lead to the production of a test set of any specific completeness. It is therefore generally necessary to use structure testing to safeguard against any inadequacies of this approach.

SELECTING TEST DATA VALUES

The best test data value to use is generally not one which is representative of those encountered in the normal operation of a system. Ideally, it should be representative of the full potential of the system *and* be capable of revealing errors. Over the years, experts have identified a number of such values.

Distinct Values

Distinct values testing involves the creation of test data using the distinct values rule: this states that:

> Every instance of every input variable, program variable or intermediate result input or computed during a test should be unique in value.

The problem which distinct values testing attacks is that of *error visibility*. One type of error which may occur in practice is the use of a wrong variable name, eg an input field rather than an output field, a wrongly subscripted variable, the wrong one of two variables with highly similar names, etc. Such errors may be termed errors of confusion. Use of the distinct values rule creates a set of circumstances in which errors of confusion *must* be reflected in test outputs.

Unless the 'oracle' (jargon), the person or thing evaluating the test output, is careless, the faults in the output, and in the software, will be recognised.

Boundary Values

Boundary value testing involves testing with pairs of data values which bracket the boundary between sets of values (of a data item) processed in different ways. Normally, the boundaries between different sets of values can be and are deduced from the specification.

If one or both of a pair of test values are processed incorrectly, it is obvious that the software is wrong. The fact that a pair of values is processed correctly does not however indicate that the software is right: it merely indicates that some conditional statement within the software jumps to the right routines for these two values. To establish that the software jumps to the right routines for an appropriate range of values, other evidence is necessary.

One possibility to be considered is that a test which ought to be an inequality has accidentally been coded as an equality. Were this to occur, the boundary value would be the only value correctly processed. To eliminate this possibility, it is desirable to combine the testing of boundary values with the use of one non-extreme value for every set of data values.

Special Values

There is no universally accepted specification of special test values. The following values are however suggested.

Zero

Mathematically zero is odd: dividing by it will not work; multiplying by it reduces any number to non-existence; adding or subtracting it is a pointless exercise.

Testing computations with one or more zero operands can identify an inability to deal with a division by zero situation, but more frequently will demonstrate that a piece of software is capable of doing something which in human, business and logical terms is nonsensical.

Blank

It is not unknown for designers to forget to protect against the omission of alphabetic or alphanumeric data resulting in silly situations during operation.

Nulling Values

Where any item of data can be zeroised or set to blank by the use of some special representation of that item, eg 'NIL', the nulling value should be considered special because within the software it will need to be detected and handled by some exception routine.

ALTERNATIVE CONCEPT OF TEST CASE CONSTRUCTION AND USE

Introduction

During testing, tests are aimed at individual modules, groups of modules, programs and systems. It is tempting to believe that the various objects of test are different types of entity amd must be tested differently. However, the algorithms tested in modules are the same algorithms found in programs and systems. Also, the techniques of analysis and test data construction are essentially identical whatever is being tested.

Recognising this, one way to approach testing would seem to be to define a single, all-embracing test set adequate for testing the system as a whole and to use component parts of this test set in testing individual components of the system.

Attempting to do this could have practical benefits:

−   duplication of the analytical part of test set construction could be minimised;

−   if the thoroughness of testing could be established in the early stages, through structure testing, the thoroughness of later stages could be, to a fair extent, taken for granted;

−   a degree of consistency between unit tests should allow the output of one unit test to be input to some other unit (subject to available software) giving some early assurance that interfacing problems do not exist and saving some work associated with physical test set construction.

The approach suggested is purely hypothetical. So far as is known, it has never been put into practice. The remainder of this chapter considers some aspects of its practical application.

The Need for an Intellectual Basis

In ad hoc testing, tests can be, and often are, improvised through common sense analysis of the software under test. By contrast, the procedure outlined above attempts to approach the problem of testing components of a system with little reference to the components themselves. In such circumstances, the old 'improvisation' approach to test case construction is impossible and test case construction has to have some sound intellectual basis. The following basis is suggested.

Thorough testing demands comprehensive execution of software. This in turn demands control over the execution of software. In practice, this control can only be exercised through input (test) data. A test set which is, in all manner, representative of the data used by a system should lead to thorough testing.

The following section outlines how such a test set might be developed.

A Data-Oriented Approach to Testing

The first step has to be to identify all input data.

So far as testing is concerned, data must be thought of as any 'stimulus' external to the software under test. This is a broader definition than that sometimes used: data is that which is in files and in databases. The broader definition includes:

– file and database identifying details;

– date and time;

– job control language parameters identifying program run, disk volumes, etc;

– operator 'commands', etc;

– interrupts, etc.

Having identified all data, the next useful step is to partition each data item into clusters of equivalent values. A cluster is merely a conceptual entity, a container for all values of a data item which it is reasonable to believe will be treated identically by a piece of software.

Initially, partitioning into clusters is easy because certain distinctions, eg between valid and invalid values, are obvious. Subsequently, it can become more difficult as more obtuse distinctions are considered.

The partitioning process cannot be comprehensively demonstrated for every conceivable type of data item. The following paragraphs do however show the type of thinking necessary where certain standard types of data item are concerned.

Numeric items are easiest to deal with. Any numeric item can be thought of as a line stretching between some minimal and maximal value. So far as the system as a whole is concerned, the extent of this line will be defined by limitations of the input technology, operating system or utility routines. In other words, the line encompasses all values which can be input — irrespective of whether they are or are not valid.

Typically, in the case of a numeric data item, extreme positive and extreme negative items will be invalid. These two sets of values must be considered to be two separate clusters because their limits will be implemented by separate conditional expressions within the software and consequently they will be processed through the use of different program paths.

Within the central, valid region, positive and negative items must be clustered separately because of the possibility of inadequate handling of negative items (eg in COBOL an output may be specified as 'unsigned' resulting in a negative item being shown as positive on output).

Finally, all special values must be identified as distinct clusters. The end-product of this exercise is the identification of a number of clusters containing only one value — normally a so-called special value, and a number of continuous series of values.

From these clusters, it is possible to identify 'representative' values for the data item — these being the isolated special values, the boundary values of the series and single, non-extreme values from each series.

In the case of numeric transaction codes or 'indicators', each valid code will form a cluster because each will stimulate a different function or the execution of a different path. Any gaps in the numeric series must be considered as invalid clusters, each containing a *continuous* series of numbers. Clusters beyond the highest and lowest values and special values must be distinguished, as in the case of numeric data.

Alphabetic and alphanumeric items pose different problems.

The partitioning previously discussed is concerned primarily with the magnitude of a data item. Where alphabetic and alphanumeric items are concerned, the magnitude of a data item is its physical dimension — the length of the character string. It is suggested that strings of zero length, minimal length, maximal length and one more than maximal length constitute appropriate values for boundary testing. Blank and nulling values must be considered special values.

In respect of all data items, further values should be defined which are of inappropriate type for use in testing input routines.

The end-product of this partitioning is a register containing a set of values of each data item sufficient at least for boundary and special values testing.

The use of distinct values testing is also desirable and can be simply adopted by adding distinct values to the representative values, eliminating the random values within value series where the distinct values serve the same purpose.

Having identified the relevant data items, it is necessary to map these into inputs, records, and module interfaces,etc. This must partly be done software entity by software entity, but can partly be done for the system as a whole.

It is reasonable to start by developing representative standing files: standing files containing all representative data values in all representative combinations.

This is not too difficult because it is normally quite easy to recognise interdependencies between data items within a record.

In any system, many programs will make use of standing files. To test these programs thoroughly, it is essential not only to input all representative values, but also all representative file structures. It follows that when specifying standard files, as many structural possibilities as possible should be developed making use of representative values, and that additional records should be defined as appropriate.

Programs which input and validate raw data can be tested with data representative of invalid data and with the valid data necessary to create the specified standing files. Initially, it is not necessary to input all the data necessary to create the standing files, only that part which includes the representative values. The processing of this test set should adequately 'prove' the software's ability to distinguish between good and bad data. Subsequently, the remainder of the valid data can be input to provide test data valuable in testing the remainder of the system.

Invariably, a system will include some form of update function whose behaviour depends on the presence or absence of correspondence between the input and the standing file being updated.

In testing such programs, additional tests will need to be derived to test situations involving significant combinations of records, that is, ensuring that there is and is not a match between files. All matching situations can be tested making use of the representative standing files. To test non-matching situations however requires the introduction of additional 'non-representative' records.

Need for a Logical Expression of Test Data

Given that the test set must adopt a variety of physical forms for module testing, system testing, etc, it must initially be defined in some manner independent of physical form. This might be done by describing all representative values in a register of some sort and describing individual tests in terms of their use of these representative values, eg one test uses maxima, one minima, one random values, etc.

7 Structure Testing

INTRODUCTION

Structure testing involves utilising technology to monitor the execution of test runs in an effort to prove, by a combination of direct observation and deduction, that a piece of software has been adequately exercised.

Structure testing is merely a way of getting some feedback from the test process. This feedback is important in two respects. Firstly, it provides a means of keeping track of the test process. Secondly, it provides a driving force which stimulates the development of the test set to a nearer complete state.

Some feedback can be provided through quite simple means such as the program trace facility (provided by most compilers and operating systems) or the inclusion of print commands at strategic points in program flow. More complex monitoring however involves the use of 'instrumentation' packages or coverage analysers.

Typically two 'programs' are involved in coverage analysis. The first analyses the source text of programs and inserts subroutine calls or 'probes' at strategic points in the flow paths through the program. When, during the execution of tests, these probes are executed, essential information will be recorded either on a file or in a database.

Execution of the probe will normally simply record the fact that the probe has been executed.

The second program involved analyses the data accumulated during test execution and is generally capable of reporting the parts of the program executed and not executed and of providing some indication of the 'thoroughness' of testing in the form of 'metrics'.

It is normally necessary to accumulate information over a number of test runs to prove adequate execution. Where simpler technology is used, the information must be accumulated and consolidated by manual means. The more sophisticated technology, particularly that making use of a database, does this automatically.

THE AIMS OF STRUCTURE TESTING

In structure testing, any one of three primary test aims may be pursued. Each is associated with a 'method' of testing and with a metric.

The various aims of structure testing are all encompassed in two competing hierarchies of metrics. One is promoted by Software Research Associates, Los Angeles, California. This is the hierarchy of coverage or C metrics (TN 843 Software Research Associates; or reference 58 for an introduction). The other is promoted by Liverpool Data Research Associates, Liverpool, England. This is the hierarchy of Test Effectiveness Ratios or TERs (88).

The C metrics are more comprehensive in so far as they take account of a number of secondary or subsidiary test aims. The TER metrics however include one metric stronger than any to be found in the C metrics.

The following sections describe the various philosophies of structure testing and, in doing so, define and discuss their basic aims in some detail.

STATEMENT TESTING

The aim of statement testing is to execute all program statements.

Attempting to execute all statements seems intuitively to be a sound idea and a reasonable attempt at thorough testing. Actually, all the statements in a program *could* be executed without revealing errors even if it were riddled with errors.

The primary value of statement testing rests in the fact that conventional test-set production methods are inadequate and tend to result in up to 40% of any piece of software not being tested (executed) at all. Monitoring the execution of tests and aiming to execute all statements at least ensures that most statements are 'tested', albeit inadequately.

In pursuing this aim, some care is necessary to ensure that all code is actually tested.

Depending on the monitoring procedure used and the syntax of the programming language used it may be possible to be misled by IF-THEN-ELSE constructs. If for example, execution were monitored by the use of the COBOL TRACE facility, which indicates only the execution of paragraphs, a paragraph could be inadvertently marked as tested even though it contained an IF-THEN-ELSE construct. In practice of course only the code associated with the THEN or the ELSE could be executed.

Statement testing is associated with a metric known as the C0 or TER1 metric: this is simply the percentage of statements executed. In practice, for reasons described in the following section, it will often be impossible to execute all statements. Generally, testing of more than 85% of statements is deemed acceptable — 85% being a crude, generalised approximation of the code likely to be testable.

BRANCH TESTING

The aim of branch testing is to execute all branches within a piece of software.

The term 'branch' is open to misinterpretation. Those who are familiar with low-level programming languages may think of a branch as a type of jump instruction. In fact, the term 'branch' comes from directed graph theory.

A directed graph is merely a way of representing a network. As such, it can be used as a means of representing computer programs. In the graph shown in Figure 7.1, zeppelins represent decision points, and the arcs represent whatever joins them together. The zeppelins are known as nodes whilst the joining lines are known variously as arcs, edges or branches. The branches are also referred to as path segments — which is what they represent.

The directed graph below is best explained by relating it to the source code of a program. A node with two 'outways' corresponds to IF-THEN-ELSE. The arcs going from it correspond to the actions carried out in the THEN and ELSE situations: typically, one arc will correspond to a sequence of statements and the other will be either a sequence of statements or a transfer of control; a jump to another statement.

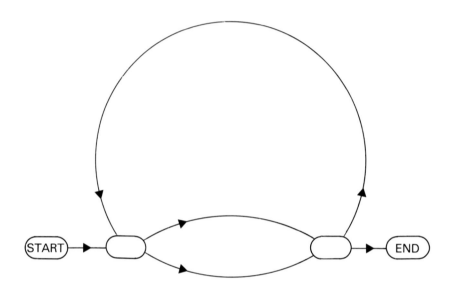

Figure 7.1   A Directed Graph

For testing to be truly thorough, it is generally believed that all viable combinations of path segments must be executed. In general, this aim is not practicable because the number of viable combinations is extremely large and may be infinite. Attempting to execute all path segments once is the lowest useful approximation to this aim.

The primary value of branch testing is that it takes account of the logical structure of software and forces the execution of both THEN and ELSE actions in IF-THEN-ELSE. This may be of more dramatic significance than it first appears. In addition to causing execution of the THEN and ELSE branches, it will often cause subsequent path segments to operate on combinations of data they may otherwise not have operated on.

In order to take account of the logical structure of software and practice branch testing, instrumentation facilities are really a necessity.

The end-products of instrumentation are typically:

- a list of the segments of code still to be executed;
- a list of the segments of code executed in this test;
- the percentage of all segments executed: this percentage is commonly known as the C1 or TER2 metric.

The C1 or TER2 metric is the driving force of branch testing, the method's aim often being expressed in terms of achieving some specific percentage of C1 coverage.

In practising branch testing, it must be recognised that it may be impossible to execute all path segments and hence achieve 100% C1 coverage.

There are a number of reasons why code may not be executable. Firstly, the links into some piece of code may have been inadvertently omitted during coding. Secondly, the program may have developed during coding in a way that makes some already produced piece of code redundant. In both these cases, non-executability is the result of errors in coding.

The third reason for non-executability is 'protective unreachability'. This occurs when code is included to deal with an 'error' situation which cannot occur (in theory) because it is dealt with in some other part of a program or system: it is associated with protection schemes in which checks are layered so that if the outermost layer fails an inner layer will still catch the fault.

The fourth explanation of non-executability is that code may be 'out of line'. For example, in COBOL, DECLARATIVES which deal with, say, errors in disk handling are not 'on' any path, they are triggered as required by input-output routines (file handlers and device handlers). Some such routines may be virtually impossible to test.

The fact that 100% execution may be infeasible provides a plausible excuse for incomplete testing. Testers must take care not to use this excuse: they must aim to execute all executable code *and* satisfy themselves and be prepared to satisfy others that what remains unexecuted at the end of test is legitimately non-executable code.

Testers must also take care when changing software during the test phase. If software under test is structurally changed by adding or deleting IFs, changing the destination of GOTOs or adding or deleting GOTOs, the test process must be restarted because the program will have been fundamentally altered and its path structure may have been more radically altered than is believed.

LCSAJ TESTING

LCSAJ testing is a comparative newcomer. Procedurally, it is virtually identical to branch testing. Technically however it differs from other structural test methods in the way it 'carves up' a program. Also, LCSAJ testing is associated specifically with the TER range of coverage measures.

The aim of LCSAJ testing is to test all LCSAJs.

LCSAJ stands for linear code sequence and jump. An LCSAJ is a rather odd unit − basically a body of code:

− through which the flow of control *may* proceed sequentially;

− which appears contiguously in the source code;

− which is terminated by a jump in the control flow.

In effect it is a contiguous, 'executable' sequence of path segments terminated by a jump instruction. It is sometimes referred to as a jump-jump segment.

In order to demonstrate the value and problems of LCSAJ testing it is necessary to provide a clearer understanding of LCSAJs than a mere definition can provide.

A particular section of code may consist of a conditional expression followed by an action to be carried out only if the conditional expression is true and by a 'common tail' which is to be carried out regardless of the truth or falsehood of the conditional expression. Such a code sequence, when considered out of context, will give rise to three LCSAJs:

− the first terminating with the conditional expression;

− the second consisting of the common tail;

− the third including the conditional expression, the conditional action and the common tail.

The diagram (Figure 7.2), symbolically representing source text, illustrates this partitioning of a program.

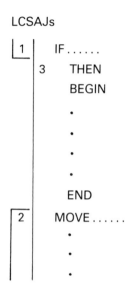

Figure 7.2   A Simple View of LCSAJs

In reality, if the code so far discussed existed in the context of other code, LCSAJs would only be formed as stated if the common tail contained no conditional expressions and terminated with an unconditional jump.

If the common tail included a conditional expression, the two LCSAJs including the common tail would split to create LCSAJs terminating with the added conditional expression and continuing with the second conditional action and possibly a second common tail. A new LCSAJ would also be formed consisting solely of the second common tail.

The diagram (Figure 7.3), symbolising source text, illustrates how such a program may be partitioned into LCSAJs.

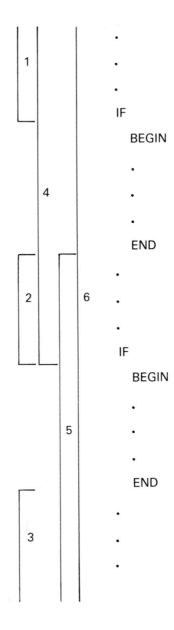

Figure 7.3   A More Realistic View of LCSAJs

From the discussion so far, it should be apparent that individual path segments may appear in many LCSAJs and consequently the number of LCSAJs *can* be considerably greater than the number of path segments.

Associated with LCSAJ testing is a hierarchy of coverage measures known as Test Effectiveness Ratios or TERs:

$$TER1 = \frac{\text{number of statements executed at least once}}{\text{total number of executable statements}}$$

$$TER2 = \frac{\text{number of branches executed at least once}}{\text{total number of branches}}$$

$$TER3 = \frac{\text{number of LCSAJs executed at least once}}{\text{total number of LCSAJs}}$$

TER1 is equivalent to C0. TER2 is equivalent to C1. TER3 is novel and is of such significance that it is considered thoroughly in later paragraphs.

Initially higher TER measures were suggested which were all of the general form:

TER(N+2) = total number of complete paths (of length N or fewer LCSAJs) tested/Total number of such paths

These measures are now seldom mentioned. Probably they prove to be of little value in practice.

As C1 is the driving force of path testing, TER3 should be the driving force of LCSAJ testing. In aiming for a high TER3, the tester is forced to consider and deal with problems arising from the *combination* of path segments.

It is obvious that long LCSAJs represent combinations of path segments. It is less obvious that short LCSAJs also represent combinations of path segments; the paths involved being *disjoint*. Essentially, the appearance of a path segment in an LCSAJ represents the execution of that path segment in some specific and potentially novel context.

It is the attention given to combination of path segments and to the execution of path segments in different contexts which makes TER3 and LCSAJ testing of considerable value. Whilst a high TER3 does not indicate that all combinations of path segments have been tested, it does indicate that a significant percentage has. Whilst it does not indicate that there are no potentially dangerous combinations which might be brought to light by operational use of the software, it does reduce the possibility considerably.

Although TER3 is a better measure of test thoroughness it cannot normally indicate true completeness of testing.

One reason for this is that LCSAJs, being composed of path segments, may, like path segments, be data-sensitive. They will therefore require to be exercised more than once. No TER measure reflects this multiple exercising of LCSAJs.

Also, the body of a loop must be demonstrated to work on data provided initially from outside the loop and on data provided subsequently from within the body of the loop.

This demands two executions of LCSAJs within the body of the loop − and LCSAJ testing does not inherently demand two executions of anything.

LCSAJ testing, in common with all test methods, is not without its practical problems.

The formation of LCSAJs depends in part on the sequence and organisation of source code, so logically there should be 'good' and 'bad' ways of organising source code with LCSAJ testing in mind. The two pieces of source text (Figure 7.4) show the problem.

Logically, the two texts have the same flow and achieve the same result, but they give rise to different LCSAJs. The reason for the difference is that in the second example, the extra unconditional 'GO TO Y' terminates an LCSAJ which would otherwise have continued, as it did in the first example.

In the case shown, the first example probably shows the better way to organise source code. This is the better approach because it more clearly shows true program paths, thus inspiring greater confidence that problems arising from the combination of path segments will be minimal.

The problem of source code organisation is arguably not that there

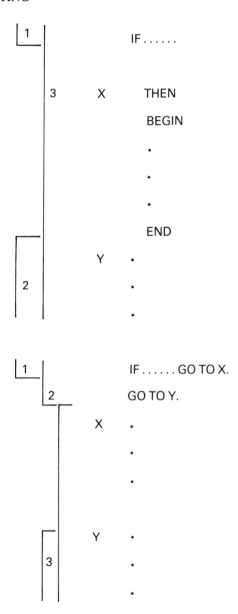

**Figure 7.4   The Organisation of Source Code and its Effect on
Partitioning into LCSAJs**

is a right and wrong way of organising source code but that at present the extent to which the effectiveness of the method and the organisation of source code are related is not known. This in turn means that the effectiveness of the method *might* not be constant and *could* in some circumstances be inadequate. It appears however that effective LCSAJ testing is consistent with 'good' structured programming and that therefore most commercial organisations should have no significant worries on this count.

Another problem of LCSAJ testing centres on 'infeasible paths'. In determining LCSAJs, the software involved takes account only of the jump structure of the program: it does not take account of the operational flow of a program. An extract from the source text of a program (Figure 7.5) helps to illustrate what is meant by this.

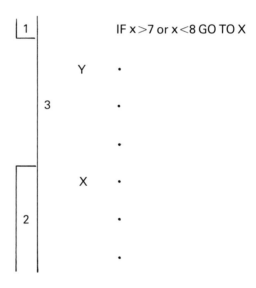

Figure 7.5   An LCSAJ Infeasible of Execution

The software involved will assume that the IF statement can evaluate to both true and false. On this understanding, it will define an LCSAJ which involves dropping through the IF statement and executing paragraphs X, Y and anything which follows. In reality, no value of x can exist (assuming x to be an integer) which will cause the IF statement to evaluate to false — so the long LCSAJ can never be executed.

A more realistic example of this phenomenon of infeasible paths involves two IF statements (shown in Figure 7.6).

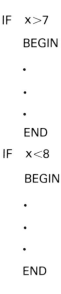

```
IF   x>7

     BEGIN

       •

       •

       •

     END
IF   x<8

     BEGIN

       •

       •

       •

     END
```

Figure 7.6   A Program Which Will Give Rise to an LCSAJ Infeasible of Execution

The software would assume that both IF statements can evaluate to false and that there is therefore a long LCSAJ involving all the text shown. This of course cannot be: any value of x which will cause the first IF statement to evaluate to false will cause the second to evaluate to true and vice versa.

One of the originators of the method, Dr Michael Hennell, suggests that commercial programs typically generate high percentages of LCSAJs incapable of execution: 40—50% of LCSAJs may represent infeasible paths. This might be seen as a problem. Dr Hennell argues that it is not much of a problem: most LCSAJs which are infeasible of execution can rapidly be seen to be infeasible — often the cause is the inclusion of mutually exclusive IF statements.

A tester could, if he so desired, easily and quickly make allowance for LCSAJs infeasible of execution simply by lowering his test objective: rather than aim for a TER3 measure of 100%, he may have to aim for TER3 = 60%. In practice, this process of adjustment is identical to that used in dealing with unreachability in statement testing. In lowering the test objective, care must be taken to avoid simply legitimising the inadequate testing which can be easily done.

The alternative approach to dealing with LCSAJs infeasible of execution is to revise the program and eliminate them. This generally improves the structure of the programs involved and can have a beneficial impact on maintenance.

Given the right source code organisation, LCSAJ testing involves testing more substantial parts of paths than does any other structural test method: it is the closest approximation to true all-path testing there is. It is possible that there is no feasible method of approximating all-path testing more closely. There is therefore a strong argument that those who claim to seek more thorough testing should consider LCSAJ testing.

8 Measuring Test Thoroughness

SEEDING/BEBUGGING

Seeding is the same as bebugging: it is a method for estimating the number of errors remaining in a piece of software and hence for determining the completeness of testing by means of statistical techniques.

The statistical principle on which seeding is based is described by Feller in 'An Introduction to Probability Theory and its Applicatons', thus:

> Suppose 1000 fish are caught in a lake and marked by red spots and released. After a while a new catch of 1000 fish is made, and it is found that 100 among them have red spots. We assume naturally that the two catches may be considered as random samples from the population of all fish in the lake. These figures would justify a bet that the true number of fish lies somewhere between 8500 and 12000.

The practice of seeding is as follows.

Having tested a program and supposedly proven it error free, the tester(s) responsible pass the program to an adversary or adversary group who insert a number of artificial errors. The tester then repeats the complete test procedure using the previously used test data.

Having run the complete procedure, the tester reports the errors detected to the adversary who establishes the number of artificial errors detected. The tester provides a total of the actual errors previously detected. In theory, the ratio of artificial errors not found to artificial errors found is approximately equal to the ratio of original errors not found to original errors found.

Seeding has many critics. They point out that program errors tend not to be randomly distributed: that they tend to centre on complex routines or on sections of code which are in some way novel to the programmer concerned: that they may also congregate on certain types of program statement. Also, the number of errors generally in a program and the number of errors seeded is, in statistical terms, small. The points made suggest that the laws of statistical probability do not in this case hold and that the theory of seeding is therefore ill-founded.

In addition to the fundamental problems already mentioned, seeding suffers from practical problems. Firstly, it is extremely difficult to seed errors which are representative of natural errors. In practice there is a tendency to seed errors which are so obvious that their detection is unavoidable, or so obscure that the chance of their detection is minimal.

A second problem is that if seeded errors are to be 'representative', they must be numerous because programmers may make many types of error. As they must be produced and inserted manually, the process of seeding can be too extensive and therefore expensive to contemplate.

The third practical problem concerns the seeding of errors which affect the flow of the program. The seeding of errors can misdirect data into routines not designed for that data and can thus create 'spurious' errors (for example when a routine to process valid data finds itself processing invalid data). Similarly, it can misdirect data away from routines containing seeded errors thus preventing their detection (for example, it might suppress the reporting of errors in input, preventing errors in the reporting routine from being detected).

The seeding of errors which affect control flow can distort error totals and provide a false picture of the errors remaining. The logical thing to do is to *not* seed errors which affect control flow. This would of course mean that seeding could 'measure' only the residual *action* errors: it would be of no value in estimating residual domain errors.

Seeding suffers from too many problems to be considered a reliable technique for evaluating test thoroughness and completeness. At best, if well practised, it may give some idea of the number of action errors remaining in software after test.

EVALUATING TEST THOROUGHNESS THROUGH REASONING

Introduction

Throughout Chapters 6 and 7, rules for thorough testing have been presented. By following these rules, one would hope to achieve thorough testing. In practice, testing is more likely to be adequate than thorough. The aim of this section is to show why this is so and thus to introduce further rules which can be used in assessing the thoroughness of testing.

The Problems of Data-Sensitive Code

The fact that a particular segment of code produces correct results once is by no means an indication that it will always do so, simply because the code involved may be data-sensitive. The following paragraph explains what is meant by this.

A sequence of code statements containing no conditional expressions is apparently unconditional and therefore capable of only one form of behaviour. In practice, although it is capable of only one operation, it can often produce more than one outcome. For example:

- it may portray all outputs as positive. Where results are positive, the outcome is correct. Where they are negative, it is in error;

- where, say, 'quantity' is multiplied by 'price', the result may be correct except where quantity or price is zero. In this case, the result may be considered wrong because the operation producing it is illogical;

- where a variable is divided by another variable, a correct result may be produced except in the case where the divisor is zero.

Ideally, any statement in a program should be tested with every 'significant' value: that is, with every value which might bring to light some defect. This is the aim underlying the partitioning of data values, and of special values testing.

It is suggested that in assessing the thoroughness of testing, it is necessary to go beyond verifying the use of special values testing, as described, and consider the more general question of whether every significant value has been input during test.

Context Sensitivity

The preceding section argues, quite reasonably, that the operation of any segment of code depends on the data it processes. The data to be processed by any segment of code is partially dependent on the data input, and partially on the processing carried out before the segment of code is reached. It is in recognition of this fact that experts seek to execute all program paths − all routes between the initial and terminal instructions of a program.

In practice, true all-path testing is impossible. Statement testing, branch testing and LCSAJ testing however try to approximate all-path testing.

By considering the question 'has each code segment been executed in every possible context?' it is possible to consider the strengths and weaknesses of the various methods, as has been done in Chapter 7, and to identify specific deficiencies in specific situations.

Testing Program Loops

This section uses the logic introduced in the preceding section to consider the thoroughness of testing of program loops.

The flow of the program in the area of a program loop can be conceptually divided into four parts. In Figure 8.1, segment a represents that which precedes execution of the loop. Segment d is that which follows the execution of the loop. Segments b and c together represent the loop itself.

In practice, b and c could be a single contiguous code sequence: a single path segment. Such a sequence can however be conceptually split into two pieces as the diagram shows. Segment b represents the function or process to be iterated and segment c represents 'administrative' code whose purpose is to allow, permit or make the

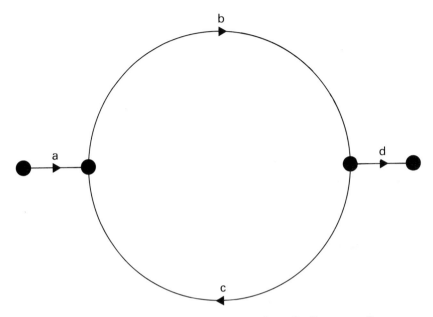

Figure 8.1 A Symbolic Representation of a Program Loop

process iterative. Typically, in segment c, the next item of data to be processed will be selected.

Obviously, the first time that segment b is executed, it depends on segment a to supply appropriate data. The second time however it depends on segment c to supply appropriate data. Executing b once only is therefore not adequate because it would fail to cause b to be executed in one representative situation—when c does the set up for the iterated process. It is with this thought in mind that experts recommend that all loops be executed twice in succession.

Further thought suggests that the value of executing looped code twice in succession is uncertain. Suppose that within the loop, a selection took place and that the loop effectively contained two paths: one to deal with each of two types of record. The diagram might be changed as shown in Figure 8.2.

The possibility exists that in normal operation the record causing the '1' path to be followed might be followed by a record which causes

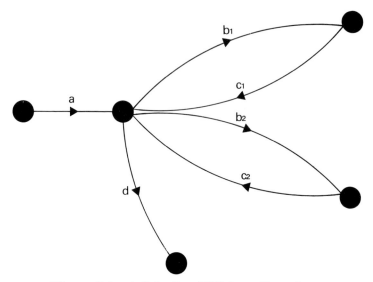

Figure 8.2   A Selection Within an Iteration

the '2' path to be followed. In test therefore, b_1 should ideally be executed after a, after c_1 and after c_2. Also, b_2 should be executed after a, after c_1 and c_2. As the number of paths through the loop increases, so thorough execution becomes more of a practical impossibility.

The above problem might be soluble through good design. The sort of schematic which might be sought is shown in Figure 8.3.

What this diagram shows is that all administrative code associated with looping has been brought together into one common tail segment. The various b segments should now be independent of each other's prior execution.

Successful operation of a particular process during the second pass through a loop indicates that execution of that process will always be successful during the second pass through the loop *only if* the second pass execution is representative of all second pass executions of the process involved. The suggested solution aims to create such circumstances by making the administrative code responsible for maintaining the iteration unconditional. What matters of course is not what is aimed at, but what is achieved. In practice, it would be

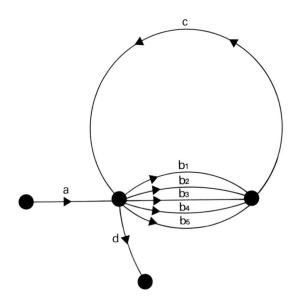

Figure 8.3 A Good Structure for a Loop

quite difficult to prove that a program is constructed according to the schematic proposed. Consequently, the suggested solution is probably of greater theoretical than practical significance.

In the longer term, it might be possible to prove that a program is consistent with the proposed schematic through the use of some form of static analysis. This could then confirm the 'reliability' of executing loops twice in succession.

There is another problem to consider.

The fact that a process is successful, when executed during the second pass through a program loop, does not guarantee that it will be successful during a third or subsequent pass of the loop: it is possible to produce a loop which gives rise to a continually varying context.

In order to guarantee that a process which is successful during the second pass of a program loop will be successful on some (any) subsequent pass, it must be shown that the second pass execution is characteristic of all subsequent pass executions: this involves proving that the operation of the administrative code which maintains the iteration has the same logical outcome under all conditions. This, it is suggested, is best proven by reasoning.

The other problem of loops is that of non-execution. In general, segment d will be executed after a,b and c, and attempting to test each path segment once will cause this sequence of paths to be executed. Possibly however b and c may not be executed in some operational run of the program. In this case, segment d would find itself operating on data originated by a rather than c: this could be difficult and could expose deficiencies in d. For this reason, it is generally recommended that a test case which causes non-execution of any loop should be included in any test set.

Loops Within Loops

All that has so far been said deals with a loop in continuous operation. In practice, a loop may be discontinuous in its operation, ie once it has executed a number of times, or until a certain condition comes about, a loop may temporarily terminate. This is of course a loop within a loop.

The problem with this phenomenon is that what follows execution of the inner loop within the outer loop could create different starting conditions when the inner loop begins executing for a second time. If the 'tail' within the outer loop contains many paths, many sets of starting conditions should in theory be created in test. In practice, this is unlikely to prove possible. In effect, it involves causing execution of all paths, using the term in the sense of a route between the initial and terminal instructions of the program. This has for some time been accepted as impossible to achieve in practice.

Summary

Observations regarding the testing of program loops are of considerable significance because, as is often said, the loop is the basis of commercial programs. Theoretically, the testing of loops in an ad hoc manner is so dubious as to be virtually valueless. Even the disciplined approach now adopted by experts is highly suspect. This involves testing non-execution and testing the execution of loops twice in succession.

There is an argument that experience proves the expert approach adequate. There is however an alternative view that of the few faults which infiltrate operational software, a considerable proportion are related to looping. The best advice which can currently be offered is essentially to test non-execution of loops and execution twice in succession (whilst bearing in mind the unreliability of such tests) and to ensure that such tests are carried out within the context of paths likely to be followed in operational use of the program. If, long-term, the approach provides acceptable levels of correctness, the approach is satisfactory. Those who demand greater levels of correctness than the approach can guarantee have no option but to move away from testing, at least as a sole means of validating code.

One approach to be considered is that of using static analysis techniques to identify 'paths of consequence', ie paths which may reveal faults resulting directly from the looping of a program. How this might be achieved is at the present time an open question.

It is also worth noting that any consideration of the problems of loop-testing involves considerable careful and thorough analysis: this suggests that verification may in some way have a part to play.

Summary of Test Aims

In addition to executing all statements, path segments or LCSAJs once, it is at least necessary to:

- test non-execution of loops;

- test each loop twice in succession;

- ensure adequate coverage of each 'path' in terms of data: that is, each 'path' must be tested with all data values likely to reveal defects.

Selection of the basic aim depends partly on the thoroughness required and partly on the expertise of the test organisation. Executing all statements is the least demanding test aim; executing all LCSAJs, the most.

Whilst these aims may be adequate in many commercial situations, they will not always be adequate. Where there are extreme requirements in respect of quality, it is desirable to consider whether each code segment has been executed in each significant context. This will probably require testing to be 'supported' by other techniques, notably static analysis and verification (either formal or informal).

9 Methods for the Future

INTRODUCTION

So far, this book has dealt mainly with techniques which are currently usable. This chapter looks to the future and describes a number of validation techniques which have not yet matured to the extent necessary for everyday commercial use.

Although the techniques described are little used today, they are still of interest, because they are likely to form or influence the basis of validation in the future. It is for that reason they have been included.

In dealing with each technique, an attempt has been made not only to describe the technique, but also to indicate its problems. For the sake of completeness, an evaluation of each technique has been included. This evaluation is of course purely the opinion of the author.

SYMBOLIC EVALUATION

Overview

Symbolic evaluation involves the use of a software package, a symbolic evaluator, to 'interpret' the source code of software and deduce the input which must be supplied to produce a required output or the output which will be produced from a given input.

In symbolic evaluation, data items are described symbolically, each symbol representing an unknown value of some data item. Outputs are specified in terms of inputs, using formulae: each formula (or set of formulae) represents the operations carried out along one path through the program: this is generally termed a path computation.

The required input of a path is described in terms of equalities and inequalities. In total these define the range of values of the input data items. Such a combination of input data items is generally termed a path domain.

The example shown in Figure 9.1 clarifies these descriptions.

Path Domain	Path Computation	
x < 7 y > 6	r = y − x	x and y are inputs r is an output
x > 6 y < 7	r = x − y	

**Figure 9.1   The Specification of Two Path Domains and their
Associated Path Computations**

Practice

Symbolic evaluation was developed for use in the validation of complex mathematical routines. This is evidenced by the research papers published on symbolic evaluation (23, 24), by its further development and by the symbolic evaluators which now exist: most are for use in validating FORTRAN or similar programs.

Initially, symbolic evaluators were intended to be used in a very simple way. Given a complex mathematical routine, a symbolic evaluator could deduce the formula *implemented*: this could then be sight-checked against the formula intended. The ability of a symbolic evaluator to specify path domains was intended to be used to identify and verify limits to the application of routines.

More advanced ways of using symbolic evaluators have now been developed; in particular, partition analysis, which is described separately.

Problems

Even where mathematical routines are concerned symbolic evaluation is not without its problems:

- Symbolic evaluation, because it relies upon interpretation of source code, may not adequately reflect execution: it may not adequately reflect limitations or peculiarities of the hardware used and oddities in the relevant compiler's interpretation of the source code.

- Calls to external routines represent a problem because the symbolic evaluator cannot evaluate source code it does not have. One approach to this problem is to 'simulate' an external routine by specifying the input which it expects, and the output it will produce given such input, using the symbols (symbolic variable names) used by the evaluator.

- Loops are a source of problems because lacking specific values for variables, the operation of the loop cannot be merely emulated. Instead, it must be deduced by a complex process of analysis (23). This is not always possible. Array handling suffers from similar problems.

- Symbolic evaluators can have difficulty in deducing what is actually going on. For example, it is hard for a human being to deduce that a loop executed x times, decrementing x by one on each iteration and constantly multiplying by x is calculating a factorial: this is well beyond the capability of an unintelligent piece of software. Initially symbolic evaluators could do little more than repeatedly substitute arithmetic expressions for variables resulting in some extremely lengthy formulae: one symbolic evaluator has been claimed to produce a formula occupying a full page of screen listing. They have now progressed and can do *some* formula simplification, but at least one symbolic evaluator has been built to get round the problem (rather than solve it) by operating interactively and requesting the human user of the system to reduce formulae for it.

— Even if a symbolic evaluator can deduce a formula, it may not be able to represent it well because the output device used, whether printer or VDU, lacks an appropriate character set and adequate positional control. This is an easily soluble problem.

To the commercial information processor, the symbolic evaluation of COBOL programs is a cause for concern. Symbolic evaluation is designed with mathematical routines in mind. COBOL programs of course tend to contain little mathematical content and consist mainly of code determining the process flow and MOVE statements which edit, concatenate and generally shift data around memory. It is hard to see how symbolic evaluation can ever be of value in this context: how can the effect of a program path, whose purpose is to assemble a record from data selected from a number of input records, ever be expressed in a formula?

Perhaps the most significant problems of all are those of obtaining and learning to use symbolic evaluation software.

Evaluation

Howden claims to have demonstrated that symbolic evaluation is more effective than conventional testing in detecting computational errors. When a variety of methods was used on twelve sample programs under controlled conditions, symbolic evaluation caused the detection of 15 errors, whilst conventional testing would reveal only nine with certainty. The programs contained 22 errors.

In evaluating such research (Howden W E, 'Symbolic Testing and the DISSECT Symbolic Evaluation System', *IEEE Transactions on Software Engineering,* July 1977), it is wise to bear in mind that 'one swallow does not make a summer'. Similarly in later experiments (47 or 49) he demonstrates that symbolic evaluation in combination with other test methods improves effectiveness by 3 to 20%.

Where mathematical routines are concerned, symbolic evaluation has its problems but none of the problems are so significant or fundamental that they make the approach useless. Here symbolic evaluation is about adequate as a technique for commercial use.

Currently, the applicability of symbolic evaluation to commercial data or information processing is not clear. In COBOL, much processing is implied in the structure and content of the DATA DIVISION. In some BASICs also there are formatting facilities which could, for example, cause negative values to be portrayed as positive. Before symbolic evaluation can be of use in information processing, it may need to be adapted to take account of 'hidden' processing implied by data descriptions. There is no obvious way in which this can be done.

Industry's alternative of course is to use symbolically evaluable languages.

It seems likely that symbolic evaluation will remain of no real value to the commercial information processor, unless there is some shift away from 'commercial' programming languages.

PARTITION ANALYSIS
Overview

One of the aims of validation is that of proving a program to be a faithful representation of its specification. In partition analysis, symbolic evaluation is used as a means of reducing both a program and its specification to a common abstract form so that they may be directly compared.

Practice

A program and its specification are both 'partitioned' by the use of symbolic evaluation. The symbolic evaluator used is a global symbolic evaluator which enumerates the calculations (path computations) carried out on all paths through the program and the 'datasets' used by every path − the path domains. Each combination of a path domain and its associated path computation constitutes a partition.

Two partition analyses result from this process: one representing the program, the other its specification.

In theory, and occasionally in practice, the equivalence of the program and specification can be established simply by cross-checking the two partition analyses. This is *partition analysis verification* at its very simplest.

Where there is no one-to-one correspondence between a partition derived from a specification and a partition derived from a program more complicated methods of verification must be adopted. At this stage, truthful people will suggest it is 'every man for himself'.

As the two analyses are compared, a third may be produced including only details of input domains. In this third analysis, the domains represented are known as procedure subdomains.

Each procedure subdomain specifies an input domain whose existence is implied in either the specification or program, or in both. If a partition derived from a specification and a partition derived from a program are identical, they will give rise to one procedure subdomain. If one of the input domains is larger than the other, two procedure subdomains will be formed: one representing that data which is processed identically by both program and specification; one representing the extra data.

So far as partition analysis verification is concerned, the merged (procedure subdomain) analysis is of no consequence: it is not used in partition analysis verification: it is merely produced as a by-product of verification. Once produced however it can be used in conventional testing.

Partition analysis testing differs from conventional testing only in so far as the object of testing is a procedure subdomain rather than a path or a function: conventional techniques are used to detect software defects.

Problems

Partition analysis is relatively new and is currently undergoing research and development (75). So far as commerce and industry is concerned, its use is currently impracticable because the symbolic evaluation software required is not readily available.

As has already been stated, symbolic evaluation of commercial programming languages is currently underdeveloped. And the symbolic evaluation of 'design languages' is a completely new field: to date, only extremely low-level specifications have been symbolically evaluated. It may therefore be some time before partition analysis becomes a practical proposition. If or when it does, its cost may be a problem.

If a program or its specification were altered during testing (possibly in response to the recognition of defects), some symbolic evaluation would have to be repeated and often, test cases would need to be changed in consequence. Given that symbolic evaluation is not the speediest of techniques, the computer and elapsed time taken by repeated symbolic evaluation could be substantial. When coupled with the cost of reconstructing test cases, this could make the use of partition analysis testing extremely expensive.

During development, change would need to be tightly controlled or the amount of symbolic evaluation and consequent test case reconstruction could easily become excessive.

Evaluation

Partition analysis testing and verification can be of no general value until various problems in symbolic evaluation can be overcome. If these can be solved and the identification of procedure subdomains automated, partition analysis testing would be little more complicated than conventional testing. Partition analysis testing would then likely be quite widely used. Partition analysis verification however is unlikely to ever be considered more than a technique to be used in extreme cases: it will be used only by a minority in proving programs whose integrity *must* be high.

DOMAIN TESTING

Overview

Domain testing is a method of reliably determining a set of test data which will bring 'domain' and boundary errors to light. It involves analysis of the program by 'mathematical methods' involving hypergeometry.

Practice

The sum total of readily available knowledge of domain testing is contained in no more than four or five papers published in journals or in the proceedings of international conferences (eg 85 or 87). These papers have the distinction of being, to the layman, amongst the least comprehensible ever written.

The central problem in domain testing is that it involves the use of a mathematical abstraction: a 'space' with more than three dimensions. This makes the method difficult for most people to understand. Recognising this, this section will ignore the detail of the method and concentrate on providing an understanding of the underlying principles.

For those who require it, Appendix 2 provides a detailed illustration of how domain testing works in two dimensions, ie when only two variables are involved.

Essentially, the method involves four steps:

- Identify path domains through symbolic evaluation;

- Analyse path domains to identify boundary segments;

- Devise test cases according to an algorithm;

- Process the test cases and identify boundary errors.

The first stage is straightforward. The remaining stages however require explanation. This is best provided through an analogy.

Imagine the path domains to be three fields of irregular shape, each bounded by a number of straight fences.

Consider the fence builder's problem: how, when building the fences, can he be sure that the fences are put up in the right places?

Essentially, the solution is to drive stakes into the ground at strategic places. A mathematician would argue that the corners of fields and the mid-points of fences are appropriate places. If the fence builder builds fences between the right stakes and builds them so that each passes as close as possible to the stakes on the correct side of the stake, he will put up the fences correctly.

The second stage of domain testing, the identification of boundary segments, is essentially concerned with finding the corners of the fields and establishing which corners are joined by fences. The third stage is essentially concerned with identifying the minimum number of stakes, to be placed at the corners of fields and the mid-points of fences, necessary to establish the correctness of the boundaries.

In domain testing, of course, the fields are sets of identically processed combinations of data items and the stakes are test cases.

Every test case deduced through the process described above is on or as near as possible to the boundary of acceptability for processing in some particular way. If the boundaries between classes of data are 'wrong' in the program, then when the test cases are processed, they will be wrongly processed and will give rise to results which, according to the specification, are incorrect.

Problems

The method involves building a multi-dimensional 'model' of a program's input space. Where two or three variables are involved, the resulting two and three dimensional models can be processed using conventional mathematics. However, where four or more variables are involved, all analysis *has* to be carried out with the aid of tensors or multi-dimensional matrices.

Many boundaries, indeed probably the majority of boundaries, will be defined through inequalities rather than equalities. This necessitates the solution of large systems of inequalities and further complicates the mathematics.

The mathematical complexity of the method is great, even for a mathematician.

Evaluation

Domain testing is aimed at the testing of complex mathematical routines rather than at the testing of information processing programs. The method is in theory valuable because it will cause the detection of all boundary errors (providing coincidental correctness does not occur). It will also cause the detection of some action errors.

The problem with domain testing is its complexity. The analysis carried out requires considerable skill: its complexity has not really been demonstrated to the full in the example provided. And the mathematical operations involved would tax even the most competent mathematician where many variables and many conditional expressions must be considered. It is suggested that no one would wish to practice domain testing by manual means. The future of domain testing therefore probably hinges on whether or not the method can be automated.

Given the complexity of the analysis and the mathematics involved, it would be unwise of anyone to await the automation of domain testing.

PROGRAM MUTATION
Overview

Program mutation is not a test method, it is a method of evaluating the thoroughness and completeness of testing. It revolves around the use of a mutation system — a computer system which operates like an interactive test harness but which when asked to test a program, generates 'mutant' programs and tests those too.

The key to understanding mutation is to understand what is meant by a mutant program: it is a program which differs from a given, supposedly correct program in only one statement — this statement differing from the original in only one respect.

Mutationists object to the process of mutation being described as the *introduction of errors* into the program. They rightly point out that some of the changes made are 'benign': they result in the same logical action being carried out in a different way. Such changed statements are 'equivalent' to the statements they replace, and the mutant programs containing them are described as equivalent programs.

Other statements do significantly change the operation of the program. Some such statements may be the correct version of statements which in the original program are incorrect. Others will of course be incorrect and will introduce errors.

Mutation is built on two logical premises:

- the given program and a mutant program must either be equivalent or at least one of them is wrong;

- if one of them *is* wrong, the test data should *show it* to be wrong.

In mutation, interest centres on mutants which when tested produce the same results as the original program. The tester must decide whether this is because the original and mutant programs are equivalent or because the test data is inadequate to demonstrate the presence of a defect.

Practice

Initially a tester is expected to feed the mutation system with test data. After each test case has been input, the original program is executed and the results displayed so that the tester may verify them as correct. When all test cases have been input, the mutation system starts to generate, compile and execute mutants. Eventually, it will provide simple statistics showing the total number of mutants, the number of live mutants and the number of dead mutants. Dead mutants are those which would not compile, would not terminate or which produce results different from those produced by the given program. Live mutants are those which cannot be distinguished from the original program.

The aim of the tester must be to eliminate (kill) live mutants by either accepting them as equivalent or by adding more test data. Obviously to eliminate live mutants, he or she needs further details of the surviving mutants (primarily, what has been changed), which the mutation system will provide.

The literature of mutation almost always describes the object to be evaluated as a program: this convention has been followed in the preceding text. In practice, however, the object evaluated is a sub-program entity: a subroutine, module or assembly of modules.

Problems

The value of a mutation system stems from the rules used by the system to create mutants. These rules are potentially also the source of a significant 'problem'.

Mutation systems use many rules: the highest number known to be used by any system is twenty-two. Some of these rules apply only to certain types of statements, eg conditional statements, and therefore generate few mutants. Others can generate phenomenal numbers of mutants.

For example, at least one mutation system includes a rule which creates a mutant by replacing a variable name by some other variable name used within the program. In total, this rule causes every variable name in every statement of the program to be replaced in turn by every other variable name used within the program.

Some statistics will demonstrate that the number of mutants generated is a problem: a 35-line program has given rise to 23,000 mutants: a 500-line program has given rise to 120,000 mutants. To compile and completely test such large numbers of mutants is obviously time consuming. Mutation runs on programs containing hundreds of statements can often best be measured in hours rather than minutes.

The resource consumption of mutation is a problem whose significance will probably dwindle – partly as a result of developments in hardware and partly through development of the mutation principle. There are at least three approaches to reducing the resource consumption of mutation.

The first is to phase the mutation process so that mutation rules can be applied one by one in descending order of cost-benefit. It is believed that Timothy Budd of the University of Arizona has developed a mutation system capable of phased operation.

The second approach is to use different, more cost-effective rules. The derivation of such rules is one topic of research into mutation. The third is to use some measure of artificial intelligence to prevent the production of equivalent programs.

Evaluation

The first reactions of most people to program mutation are often negative: in this context, the time taken by mutation and its computer cost are often seen as the major problems. What must be recognised however is that program mutation is still undergoing research and development. To date, all the mutation systems which have been built have been built by researchers simply so that their use and value could be researched. Research is continuing and will make mutation systems more acceptable to commerce and industry. Technology too is constantly advancing and no doubt technological development will play its part in eliminating time and cost problems.

In the future, program mutation could well become an attractive means of evaluating test completeness.

STATIC ANALYSIS

It is possible to *deduce* the existence or possible existence of errors in software simply by analysing or reasoning about its source code.

Compilers do this in a limited way: they detect syntax errors, undeclared variables, some unreachable statements. Programmers also do this in a limited way: they can detect uninitialised variables, etc. Now software systems (static analysers) have been built to do this in a potentially more exhaustive manner.

One type of static analyser concerns itself with procedure flow. In essence, such an analyser breaks the source code into segments (path segments) and examines the relationships between segments to establish that:

− there are no segments which cannot be executed;

− there are no paths which do not reach a 'STOP' statement.

Such analysers are commonly built into structural testing software.

A second type of analyser concerns itself with data flow. It can detect undeclared variables, uninitialised variables, variables set and not used, or used and not set, etc.

A third type of analyser now coming into use concerns itself with 'information flow'. So far as can be ascertained, this type of analyser implements 'cause-effect graphing' and shows what data is used in producing what results. One would expect such an analysis to provide a clearer understanding of a program, during test, and subsequently to be of value in evaluating the impact of program changes.

Problems

Virtually all analysers need to take account of process flow. In determining the flow paths from statement to statement, they invariably concern themselves only with whether or not jump instructions exist which could connect statements together: they do not concern themselves with the question of whether a particular jump could ever be executed: whether the specific values of data which would cause a particular jump would ever occur.

Given this fact, a problem should be obvious. Of all the paths considered by a static analyser, some will be infeasible because some jumps which it is assumed can be made, in fact, cannot.

All types of analyser are in limited supply, ie they exist only for certain computers and for processing programs written in certain languages. Organisations using large American computers and Fortran or Pascal probably have the best choice.

Evaluation

There is little which can now be achieved by free-standing static analysis software which cannot be achieved by dynamic testing. And there are problems of cost and of the detection of infeasible paths which ideally need solving. This means that static analysis is as yet not broadly acceptable to commerce and industry.

Static analysis however is probably the most promising approach for the future. The explanation of this statement is simply that to work with programs and to validate them, people need information: static analysers can provide a wealth of information. Probably, we have as yet no more than scratched the surface where static analysis is concerned.

FORMAL VERIFICATION

Overview

When the term 'verification' is used as jargon it means the proving of program correctness by *reasoning* about the program and its specification. Verification depends considerably on the use of formal logic and therefore appeals to a rather special and limited group of people.

A question of some significance is, what does verification prove. Initially, verification was intended as, and was described as, a means of proving a program 'correct'. In practice, program verification is a means of proving the internal consistency of a program and of proving it consistent with its specification. This is a rather limited view of correctness which falls well short of correctness in the eyes of the user.

Practice

Verification really started in earnest in the mid-sixties when, in 1967, R W Floyd produced a paper entitled 'Assigning meanings to programs'. In this paper he introduced the concept of 'invariant assertions'.

Invariant assertions are at the heart of one method of program proving. In this method, a program is divided into 'segments'. Assertions are made relating to the state of program variables between segments. They are described as invariant because by convention they should always hold true when that point in execution is reached.

The proof of the program is carried out in steps, each one seeking to prove that the assertions following a segment of code hold, assuming the assertions preceding the segment to be true.

At the extremes of a program path, assertions deal with input and expected output (or with the initial and final state) of the program. Consequently, the effect of the verification process is to establish a 'chain of proof' linking input and output. Such a chain can, in theory, only be established if the program is internally consistent and consistent with both input and output. This is the proving of 'partial' correctness.

A potential problem with this method of proving programs is that a proof step may be, as mathematicians say, vacuously true: correct in logic but not in reality. A proof step will be vacuously true if it is proven on the basis of false assertions or if the sequence of statements does not terminate. The existence of such proof steps would permit a program to be proven 'consistent' even though it was in reality 'incorrect'. These problems must be overcome by a second proving stage, the result of which is to prove 'total' correctness.

If verification were an entirely manual process it would be laborious, time-consuming and error-prone. Recognising this, researchers have sought to automate the process. Initially, the aim was to fully automate the proving aspect of verification, leaving human beings with the limited task of specifying assertions.

In recent years, however, it seems to have been generally recognised that full automation is not so desirable even if it is feasible. More recent verification systems therefore tend to be semi-automatic. These accept guidance on proof strategies to be adopted, additional information concerning the 'problem domain', and will refer some difficult proof steps to the human verifier.

Problems

What is 'total' correctness in the eyes of a verifier is not total correctness in the eyes of most people because verification takes no account of the extent to which the operation of the software depends on the compiler and the hardware used. It seems plausible to suggest that such deficiencies could be overcome, perhaps by a third stage proving process, perhaps by defining the behaviour of the programming language used, in machine-dependent terms. Such developments are probably not worthy of consideration until verification as currently defined has become a reasonably simple, ie automatic, process.

One persistent problem has been the limitation of size: verification has only been practicable where small software entities are involved. Advances in the automation of verification will eventually eliminate this problem.

Evaluation

Verification is currently of limited interest to commerce and industry and is a method for a minority: it is too complex and too laborious to be widely used. In time, verification may come into limited use in commerce and industry, but only as a means of proving the components of a system which are critical or which cannot be adequately validated by other means.

The author's view is that so far as formal verification is concerned, research is and will remain more important than practice. Even if formal verification never comes into significant use, research into formal verification will have taught us a lot about how programs work, how components fit together and what the basic problems of validation are. This basic understanding will probably ultimately be of greater value than any resulting formal verification method.

TEST MONITORING

In reference 52, W E Howden discusses program mutation and the manner in which it recognises errors of confusion: errors of confusion are errors which involve the use of a wrong variable in a program statement.

Using program mutation, such errors are recognised by systematically using every variable name in place of each variable name in each program statement. Test data should be sufficiently sensitive to detect the use of the deliberately introduced wrong variable names. If it is not, then it is not sufficiently sensitive to establish whether the original variable name was right or wrong.

Howden suggests that where this type of error is concerned, program mutation involves using a sledge hammer to crack a nut. The alternative which Howden proposes involves the use of a specialised test monitoring system. This system will monitor the execution of tests and detect the use of non-distinct values for variables.

The premise on which the system is based is that only where two variables always share a common value is detection of an error of confusion impossible. In effect all that the system does is ensure that the distinct values rule is applied properly and adequately. The value of the system is that it causes the distinct values rule to be applied and it *proves* that it has been applied thus creating confidence in testing.

Potentially, the idea of execution monitors can be extended.

One type of error which is difficult to detect is a boundary error. Boundary errors occur because of incorrect conditional expressions. An execution monitor could examine the data evaluated by a conditional expression and deduce the alternative expressions which would be acceptable given the test data. Only when all alternatives have been eliminated could a conditional statement be considered adequately exercised. Such a monitor would cause the application of rules derived from error-sensitive test case analysis (32) and prove that these rules had been applied.

A third type of monitor could 'snapshot' the data (logically) within the program at strategic points in procedural flow, eg immediately following any input and at each and every point of termination, and maintain a record of the classes of data processed. The tester's aim would be to maximise the number of classes processed. Such a monitor would in part overcome the deficiencies of structure testing with regard to data-sensitive code, but unless it took account of relationships between data items it could not of itself cause execution of all path segments. The use of this monitor and structure testing techniques could be complementary.

All of the monitors discussed are 'pie in the sky'. None yet exists. They could be produced given the will.

Whether such monitors would prove attractive in use is impossible to say without at least some idea of the construction and use of such an aid. It is suggested however that monitors such as these are worthy of research.

10 Conclusion

Recently, the author's six year old son asked why days grow longer and shorter during the year. In answering, the author described how the Earth revolves around the Sun, how the Earth spins on its axis and how the Earth's axis tilts backwards and forwards towards the Sun.

The boy refused to accept the explanation. If the Earth were moving, there would be noise, vibration and rushing winds. And people would be thrown outwards as they are on fairground rides. The boy reached a wrong conclusion because he did not have all the necessary information.

Is a tester's conclusion that a piece of software is correct any different to the little boy's conclusion that the Earth is static? To even consider this question it is necessary to know on what facts and assumptions and on what reasoning the conclusion was reached.

In practice, even many testers do not have this information. Where, within a tester's mind, there should be a clear understanding, there is often an intellectual minestrone in which facts, assumptions and irrelevant observations float aimlessly around. Hopefully, this book will help testers bring some order to this chaos and expose the tester's reasoning in all its glory.

The reader may feel in reading the later chapters of this book that he has watched a constant succession of spanners being thrown into the works and consequently may have gained the impression that the book is 'negative'. In fact, it is not. It is not the tester's job to reach half-baked conclusions − anyone can do that. What the tester seeks is the truth, and as Sherlock Holmes is reputed to have remarked "Having excluded all other possibilities, what remains must be the truth". For a tester, or a detective, to be negative is to be positive.

Finally, it is worth remarking that in proving correctness, the tester is marshalling information. His conclusion can be no better than his information and will often be worse, simply because his reasoning ability is imperfect.

In the long term, the best prospect for improving the reliability of correctness testing is research and development − research and development aimed at:

− establishing the right information on which to base conclusions concerning correctness;

− establishing the right way to interpret information;

− automating the collection and interpretation of this information.

The prospect of automation may frighten some testers just as it frightens office workers and production-line staff. It should not. The computing world is full of problems to solve, full of challenges to which testers can apply themselves. Using a computer to do the simple, tedious, dirty-work of testing is a way of finding time to address these challenges.

Appendix 1
Bibliography

Most of the articles and papers in this bibliography were obtained from the British Lending Library.

1   *ANSI/IEEE 730-1984: IEEE Standard for Software Quality Assurance Plans*
    See reference 15.

2   *BS 5887: 1980: Code of Practice for Testing of Computer-Based Systems*
    This British Standard deals with the testing of computer-based systems on a broad and mainly procedural level. It is not a document for those interested in the 'thoroughness' or 'reliability' of testing.

3   *ANSI/IEEE 829-1983: Standard for Software Test Documentation*
    This specifies the information content of test documentation rather than its detailed form. Many organisations would feel the documentation suggested is too complete.

4   'Progress in Software Engineering: Part 1', *EDP Analyzer,* Vol. 16, No. 2, February 1978
    An all-embracing article covering requirements analysis, design, construction and quality assurance of programs. Essentially the article is an 'introduction' only.

5   'Workshop Report: Software Testing and Test Documentation',
     Computer, Vol. 12, No. 3, March 1979, 98-107
     This is written by a string of well-known authorities. The report
     is of interest because it so concisely states the problems of
     testing and gives an appreciation of the 'state-of-the-art'.
     Although old, it is still highly relevant. Much of the material
     presented at the workshop has appeared in various publications
     and is included in this bibliography.

6   Adrion W R, Branstad M A and Cherniavsky J C, *Validation,
     Verification and Testing of Computer Software*, NTIS Report
     PB81-167074, 1981
     A 66-page report which outlines current ideas and available
     techniques and technology in the field of validation. The
     treatment of some techniques is of necessity superficial due
     to the size of the report. It could be argued that for the
     commercial organisation the report is wrongly balanced,
     dealing in more detail with the less usable techniques and
     technology.

7   Akers S B, 'Test Generation Techniques', *Computer*, Vol. 13,
     No. 3, March 1980, 6-15
     Deals with the testing of VLSI circuits and is therefore of little
     interest to the software practitioner.

8   Allen B, 'Idealism in Computer Programming', *Computerworld
     UK*, 9 December 1981, 16, 18, and reading list
     A polemic of interest only because it explains the limitations
     of formal program verification.

9   Andrews D M and Benson J P, 'An Automated Program Testing
     Methodology and its Implementation', *Proceedings 5th
     International Conference on Software Engineering*, 9-12 March
     1981, San Diego, California, 254-261
     Understanding of this paper depends on a knowledge of
     complexes and search algorithms. The basic principle of the
     automated strategy is to insert executable assertions into the
     code under test and use feedback about assertion violation to
     drive the Adaptive Tester (a piece of software developed in
     connection with ballistic missile defence systems).

10   Bauer J A and Finger A B, 'Test Plan Generation Using Formal

Grammars', *Proceedings 4th International Conference on Software Engineering*, 17-19 September 1979, Munich, Germany, 425-432

This is concerned with the testing of telephone switching and similar systems. It describes a procedure, based on automata theory, for generating a test plan from a description of functional requirements. The procedure is automated and the resulting plan is used to drive a test harness.

11   Belford P C and Berg R A, 'Central Flow Control Software Development: A Case Study of the Effectiveness of Software Engineering Techniques', *Proceedings 4th International Conference on Software Engineering, 17-19 September 1979, Munich, Germany, 85-93

This paper is most interesting for the facts and figures it contains which are useful background information and may be useful in 'estimating'.

12   Bicevskis J, Borzovs J, Straujums U, Zarins A and Miller E F, 'SMOTL − A System to Construct Samples for Data Processing Program Debugging', *IEEE Transactions on Software Engineering, Vol. SE-5, No. 1, January 1979, 60-66

SMOTL originates from Riga, Latvia, USSR. It analyses data processing programs and constructs test sets which exercise every branch outcome.

13   Bowen J B, 'A Survey of Standards and Proposed Metrics for Software Quality Testing', *Computer*, Vol. 12, No. 8, August 1979, 37-42

The article is based on experience of military systems and is therefore biased towards real-time working. Nevertheless, it is likely to be of general interest to those concerned with the measurement or evaluation of software quality. The procedures for testing two military systems are outlined.

14   Branstad M A, Cherniavsky J C and Adrion W R, *Validation, Verification and Testing for the Individual Programmer,* NTIS Report PB80-166960, 1980

A 23-page report aimed at one-man software development organisations. It is clear and concise to those who know all about validation, verification and testing. Non-experts may not know all the terminology used and may therefore find it less clear. What is presented is essentially a strategy and the reader is sometimes forced to say "You tell me I should do this, now tell me how!"

15   Buckley F, 'A Standard for Software Quality Assurance Plans', *Computer*, Vol. 12, No. 8, August 1979, 43-48, 50
This describes the efforts made by the IEEE to produce a standard for quality assurance plans and includes a draft of the proposed standard. Both the article and standard are valuable primarily to those with an interest in standards and/or the documentation of plans.

16   Budd T A, Lipton R J, Sayward F G and DeMillo R A, 'The Design of a Prototype Mutation System for Program Testing', *AFIPS Conference Proceedings – National Computer Conference 1978*, 5-8 June 1978, Anaheim, California, 623-627
This describes PIMS (Portable Interactive Mutation System) and its use. Also, it describes how certain classic types of error are recognised as a result of mutation. Finally, it describes the authors' plans for the future (so far as mutation is concerned). It is essentially a readable paper for practical people.

17   Budd T A, 'Mutation Analysis: Ideas, Examples, Problems and Prospects', *Computer Program Testing*, B Chandrasekaran and S Radicchi (Eds), (North-Holland, 1981), 129-148
This is entirely concerned with 'program mutation'. It is thorough and faithful to its title. Some detailed sections may prove difficult for the uninitiated.

18   Carey R and Bendick M, 'The Control of a Software Test Process', *Proceedings Computer Software and Applications Conference (COMPSAC)*, 8-11 November 1977, Chicago, 327-333
This paper presents a software testing and quality assurance 'technology' which maintains traceability from requirements specification to system test. The approach was developed for use in connection with military software. It seems to be designed also with real-time software in mind. The basic principle seems to be to represent the operation of the software as a network of 'threads' each defined as an input, process and output. Initially, these threads are derived from a requirements specification. Subsequently, processes are

described both in terms of paragraphs of the requirements specification and in terms of 'programs'. An approach to the control of test activity is also outlined.

19   Celentano A, Ghezzi C and Liguori F, 'A Systematic Approach to System and Acceptance Testing', *Computer Program Testing*, B Chandrasekaran and S Radicchi (Eds), (North-Holland, 1981), 279-287
      The approach in question is not a new approach, but rather, it organises traditional activities into a systematic framework.

20   Ceriani M, Cicu A and Maiocchi M, 'A Methodology for Accurate Software Test Specification and Auditing', *Computer Program Testing*, B Chandrasekaran and S Radicchi (Eds), (North-Holland, 1981), 301-325
      This is concerned with test documentation and test planning. In part it describes a Honeywell system — Testdoc. It is well worth reading.

21   Chen W T, Ramamoorthy C V and Huang S T, 'Automated Techniques for Static Structural Validation of Programs', *Proceedings Computer Software and Applications Conference (COMPSAC)*, 8-11 November 1977, Chicago, 628-634
      This paper concerns itself with the technicalities of static analysis, eg how can a loop without exit be detected? For the man in the street it is less than easy to follow because it has to deal with the manipulation of arrays which represent directed graphs and because the authors' English is just a little less than perfect. One interesting section deals with automated comparison of the structure of a program with the structure of its flowchart: so far as is known, nothing of significance has resulted from this idea.

22   Cicu A, 'The Quality of a Computer Program: The User View and the Software Engineer View', *Computer Program Testing*, B Chandrasekaran and S Radicchi (Eds), (North-Holland, 1981), 241-249
      This is concerned with quality and the qualities which constitute quality. The paper is extremely tenuously connected with testing. Not everyone would agree with the author's views.

23   Clarke L A and Richardson D J, 'Symbolic Evaluation Methods

– Implementation and Applications', *Computer Program Testing*, B Chandrasekaran and S Radicchi (Eds), (North-Holland, 1981), 65-102

This is extremely thorough and comprehensive but is probably of greater value to those who wish to build a symbolic evaluator than those who wish to buy and use one.

24   Darringer J A and King J C, 'Applications of Symbolic Execution to Program Testing', *Computer*, Vol. 11, No. 4, April 1978, 51-60

This outlines the utility and method of working of symbolic execution systems. Darringer and King are symbolic execution enthusiasts; and it shows: references to problems and difficulties in the construction and use of symbolic execution systems almost pass unnoticed. The article is not for the layman: a working knowledge of logic is required.

25   Degano P and Levi G, 'Software Development and Testing in an Integrated Programming Environment', *Computer Program Testing*, B Chandrasekaran and S Radicchi (Eds), (North-Holland, 1981), 251-263

This is a good paper for those with an interest in the future.

26   DeMillo R, Lipton R J and Sayward F G, 'Hints on Test Data Selection: Help for the Practising Programmer', *Computer*, Vol. 11, No. 4, April 1978, 34-41

Few hints included. In the main, this article is concerned with 'program mutation': it deals with the principles rather than with practice. It ends by emphasising the value of 'experience' in testing and seems to suggest that experience is the best knowledge base at the time of writing.

27   Duran J W and Ntafos S, 'A Report on Random Testing', *Proceedings 5th International Conference on Software Engineering*, 9-12 March 1981, San Diego, California, 179-183

This includes some mathematics which only those who understand probability theory will follow. It argues that testing with random inputs is more effective than is generally believed. However, the random inputs used are not so random.

28   Fagan M E, 'Design and Code Inspections to Reduce Errors in Program Development', *IBM Systems Journal*, Vol. 15, No. 3, 1976, 182-211

The authoritative article on inspections.

29 Fairley R E, 'Tutorial: Static Analysis and Dynamic Testing of Computer Software', *Computer*, Vol. 11, No. 4, April 1978, 14-23
Fairley was once involved in the design and development of an experimental 'automated testing system'. The back half of this article describes this system in fairly concrete terms. The front half of the article is more general, of broader interest, and includes some thought provoking statements, eg specifications are a testing problem. Parts of the article may be interpreted as instructive or definitive: some such parts may not accord with the common view.

30 Fairley R E, 'Software Testing Tools', *Computer Program Testing*, B Chandrasekaran and S Radicchi (Eds), (North-Holland, 1981), 151-186
This provides a comprehensive overview of tools useful throughout the software life cycle. It includes sufficient detail of individual tools to make it well worth reading. Considerable attention is given to the ADA support environment.

31 Fischer K F, 'A Test Case Selection Method for the Validation of Software Maintenance Modifications', *Proceedings Computer Software and Applications Conference (COMPSAC)*, 8-11 November 1977, Chicago, 421-426
This paper presents a method of selecting test cases for use in testing maintenance modifications. Essentially, the method involves cross-referencing test cases and the path segments they test. Path analysis techniques are then used to identify path segments reachable from the changed path segments, and test cases which exercise both the changed and reachable segments are identified from the cross-reference. The necessity of automation of this process is stressed.

32 Foster K A, 'Error Sensitive Test Case Analysis (ESTCA)', *IEEE Transactions on Software Engineering*, Vol. SE-6, No. 3, May 1980, 258-264
This is interesting. It suggests rules on which the construction of test cases may be based. The procedure for developing these rules is however not made too obvious.

33 Gannon C, 'A Verification Case Study', *Proceedings of the AIAA*

Computers in Aerospace Conference, 1977, 349-353
This describes the Jovial Automated Verification System, its
software design and development, and its testing. JAVS includes
dynamic testing facilities, and facilities for static analysis of
source text and structure. It is oriented towards path testing
and provides for instrumentation of programs as a means of
assessing test coverage. After testing, the residual error rate
for the JAVS system itself was 0.03% of the number of source
statements. If the system were based on the use of any language
but JOVIAL, it would be extremely useful.

34   Gannon C, 'Error Detection using Path Testing and Static
Analysis', *Computer*, Vol. 12, No. 8, August 1979, 26-31
This reports an experiment to compare the capability of static
analysis and path testing techniques. Arguably, the experimental
method is biased in favour of path testing so empirical data
must be interpreted with care. Includes useful information
related to inspection and the effort required to detect errors.
A clear conclusion is that the techniques considered are
complementary.

35   Geiger W, Gmeiner L, Trauboth H and Voges U, 'Program
Testing Techniques for Nuclear Reactor Protection Systems',
Computer, Vol. 12, No. 8, August 1979, 10-18
A good description of high-technology testing: static analysis,
dynamic analysis, symbolic execution and path testing are all
used. Reliance on these techniques is reduced by formal
specification, use of standards and duplexing (or in this case
triplexing) of hardware and software. Outlines the validation
of four other reactor systems.

36   Ghezzi C, 'Levels of Static Program Validation', *Computer
Program Testing*, B Chandrasekaran and S Radicchi (Eds),
(North-Holland, 1981), 27-34
This is a useful overview of static program validation. It shows
how the extent to which a program can be validated without
execution depends on the programming language used.
Discusses how static checking tools can be integrated in a
coherent development system (with the aid of syntax-tree
representation).

37   Goodenough J B and Gerhart S L, 'Toward a Theory of Test

Data Selection', *IEEE Transactions on Software Engineering*, Vol. SE-1, No. 2, June 1975

This is perhaps the most quoted article in the field of testing. Its most important part provides definitions of *reliable* and *valid* tests. It is this section which causes the paper to be so frequently quoted. Unfortunately for many, the various definitions are developed and presented with the aid of formal logic; so the text cannot be considered light reading.

38   Glass R L, 'Real-Time: The "Lost World" of Software Debugging and Testing', *Communications of the ACM*, Vol. 23, No. 5, May 1980, 264-271

A subjective interpretation of 'what's wrong in the field of real-time testing'. Not helpful to those dealing with day-to-day problems.

39   Glass R L and Noiseaux R A, *Software Maintenance Guidebook*, (Prentice-Hall, 1981)

This is not an impressive publication: it discusses a lot but perhaps teaches little.

40   Haley A and Zweben S, 'Module Integration Testing', *Computer Program Testing*, B Chandrasekaran and S Radicchi (Eds), (North-Holland, 1981), 289-299

This paper demonstrates a need for integration testing of supposedly correct modules and suggests that such integration testing can be well-achieved by domain testing.

41   Hartwick R D, 'Test Planning', *AFIPS Conference Proceedings – National Computer Conference 1977*, 13-16 June 1977, Dallas, Texas, 285-294

Where dealing with quality administration (planning control, documentation) this paper is very good. It contains a section on quality assurance techniques which is not so good; perhaps it is dated. The paper's only drawback is that 'americanisms' abound.

42   Hennel M A, 'Management of Validation and Testing', *Infotech State of the Art Report on Life Cycle Management*, Series 8, No. 7, 86-100

Some people would question the structure of this paper: it seems to be just a series of sections assembled in no special

order. Some people would question the author's style: he seems
to adopt an aggressive attitude. Nevertheless, the author has
got his facts right and his opinions are more than justified.
For managements who want to know what they should be
doing, rather than how they should do it, this paper is a must.

43   Herndon M A and Keenan A P, 'Analysis of Error Remediation
     Expenditures During Validation', *Proceedings 3rd International
     Conference on Software Engineering*, 10-12 May 1978, Atlanta,
     Georgia, 202-206
     This paper presents an analysis of the cost of error remediation
     during validation for only one system: a real-time
     communications system. The analysis clearly shows that
     foreshortening program and integration testing did not, in this
     case, pay: 58% of errors detected were programmer errors
     which *should* have been detected prior to validation. Analyses
     relating cause, impact and cost of error are presented and are
     themselves interesting.

44   Holthouse M A and Hatch M J, 'Experience with Automated
     Testing Analysis', *Computer*, Vol. 12, No. 8, August 1979, 33-36
     Related to the use of a software package to determine the
     coverage achieved during branch (path) testing. Indicates that
     total coverage may be impossible to achieve and explains why
     this is. Describes problems in testing loops and suggests non-
     execution of a loop must be tested. Suggests that machine
     utilisation in path testing at system level is excessive and
     outlines a more cost-effective strategy. Suggests that errors of
     omission must be recognised by functional testing.

45   Holthouse M A and Lybrook C W, 'Improving Software Testing
     in Large Data Processing Organisations', *AFIPS Conference
     Proceedings — National Computer Conference 1981*, 4-12 May
     1981, Chicago, Illinois, 353-359
     This describes why, how and with what success Chemical Bank
     (New York) developed their approach to testing.

46   Howden W E, 'Reliability of the Path Analysis Testing Strategy',
     IEEE Transactions on Software Engineering, Vol. SE-2, No.
     3, September 1976
     This records an attempt to 'calculate' the reliability of path

testing using set theory and logic. It is of no real value to dp
people in commerce and industry.

47   Howden W E, 'Reliability of Symbolic Evaluation', *Proceedings
      Computer Software and Applications Conference (COMPSAC)*,
      1977, Chicago, 442-447
      This describes an experiment. Six programs were tested using
      various methodologies: path testing, branch testing, structured
      testing, special values testing and various methods of static
      analysis in addition to symbolic evaluation. Howden concludes
      that the use of symbolic evaluation in testing may improve test
      reliability by up to 20%.

48   Howden W E, 'Theoretical and Empirical Studies of Program
      Testing', *IEEE Transactions on Software Engineering*,
      Vol. SE-4. No. 4, July 1978, 293-298
      This is concerned with the selection of reliable test methods.
      It reports two studies which adopt different approaches to
      assessing test method reliability. The first (theoretical) approach
      involves characterising the circumstances in which correctness
      can be proven by the use of some particular method. The
      second (empirical) approach involves assessing the reliability
      of existing testing techniques by experimentation. The
      theoretical part of the article is more readable to those with
      a knowledge of set theory and polynominal interpolation.
      Howden suggests that the empirical approach is of greatest
      practical benefit.

49   Howden W E, 'An Evaluation of the Effectiveness of Symbolic
      Testing', *Software — Practice and Experience*, Vol. 8, No. 4,
      July-August 1978, 381-397
      This reports research carried out by Howden and his colleagues.
      Whilst being concerned primarily with the effectiveness of
      symbolic testing, it includes useful descriptions and data
      concerning a number of other testing techniques. Concludes
      that no one testing technique is sufficient and adds that
      symbolic testing could improve test reliability by as little as
      3-4% or as much as 10-20%. Suggests that research into the
      cost-effectiveness of symbolic testing is desirable.

50   Howden W E, 'Life-Cycle Software Validation', *Infotech State*

of the Art Report on Life Cycle Management, Series 8, No. 7, 101-116
Subsequent to publication this paper was revised and reprinted in *Computer.* See reference 54.

51 Howden W E, 'Functional Program Testing', *IEEE Transactions on Software Engineering,* Vol. SE-6, No. 2, March 1980, 162-169
Howden describes an approach to functional (black-box) testing of mathematical software and claims it to be more reliable than structural testing. The approach suggested is not guaranteed to test thoroughly and some skill is required to identify and fill-in gaps in the approach. Arguably, the success of this functional testing approach was due more to the considerable skill of Howden and his colleagues than to any 'formal method'. Comparisons with structural testing are unfair because it is assumed that structural testing is practised in a 'thoughtless' manner. Potentially, what Howden has demonstrated is how much 'education' can contribute to testing.

52 Howden W E, 'Completeness Criteria for Testing Elementary Program Functions', *Proceedings 5th International Conference on Software Engineering,* March 1981, San Diego, California, 235-243
This starts well and ends well, but the middle section may be difficult for computer non-scientists. It includes rules which could be of value in test case construction and proposes the development of a (so far as is known) novel test monitor. The rules may seem familiar to those with knowledge of distinct values testing and ESTCA.

53 Howden W E, 'Errors, Design Properties and Functional Program Tests', *Computer Program Testing,* B Chandrasekaran and S Radicchi (Eds), (North-Holland, 1981), 115-127
Howden makes the point that functional program testing can now be carried out systematically. When approached in this way, functional program testing deserves to be considered as complementary to more traditional 'white-box' methods. Considerable attention is paid to the role and adequacy of formal design statements in testing.

54 Howden W E, 'Life-Cycle Software Validation', *Computer,* Vol. 15, No. 2, February 1982, 71-79

This sketches an integrated, life-cycle-long approach to validation. The most interesting sections are those dealing with requirements specifications and design specifications. They indicate that Howden is thinking of structured design in relation to functional testing.

55   Huang J C, 'Program Instrumentation and Software Testing', *Computer,* Vol. 11, No. 4, April 1978, 25-32
     This explains the concept of instrumentation and outlines the various possible uses of instrumentation in testing. A knowledge of flow graphs and finite state theory is an advantage to the reader.

56   Lauesen S, 'Debugging Techniques', *Software—Practice and Experience,* Vol. 9, No. 1, January 1979, 51-63
     A practical article. It advocates the use of top-down testing, the inclusion of diagnostic print statements in a program and the use of both path and functional testing. It puts everything in perspective by describing the validation of an 8-pass compiler. The problems of validating real-time systems are considered. The final section includes some useful 'rules of thumb', eg expect one error in every twenty program statements.

57   Lyon G, *COBOL Instrumentation and Debugging*, NTIS Report PB-275 513, 1978
     This 27-page report devotes 15 pages to the full text of a program. Most of the 10-page report proper is concerned with the incompetence of the execution timing facilities of one debugging package. The standard of authorship is not good. In total, the report has little to commend it.

58   Miller E F, 'Program Testing: Art Meets Theory', *Computer,* Vol. 10, No. 7, July 1977, 42-51
     Miller is a proponent of path testing, so not surprisingly this article is mainly concerned with path testing. It explains 'coverage measures' and some of Howden's conclusions on the reliability of path testing. A section on current developments may be of interest to the uninformed. The article is useful but is to some extent out of date.

59   Miller E F, 'Experience with Industrial Software Quality Testing', *Computer Program Testing*, B Chandrasekaran and S Radicchi

(Eds), (North-Holland, 1981), 265-277
This is a good introduction to modern test methods particularly for people with little time. It is concise, pragmatic and adequately detailed.

60 Miller E F, Henderson J B and Mapp T E, 'A Software Test Bed: Philosophy, Implementation and Application', *Computer Program Testing*, B Chandrasekaran and S Radicchi (Eds), (North-Holland, 1981), 231-237
In the main this article is concerned with 'demonstrating' the 'Interactive Test Bed', which is what its name implies.

61 Miller E F and Howden W E (eds and contributors), *Tutorial: Software Testing and Validation Techniques* (IEEE Computer Society 1978)
A compendium of important papers and articles with some original material from Miller and Howden. It is still a valuable publication to those seeking information rather than simple solutions to day-to-day problems. Includes references 28, 37, 46, 49, 58, 68 and 80.

62 Mullin F J, 'Software Test Management', *Proceedings Computer Software and Applications Conference (COMPSAC)*, 8-11 November 1977, Chicago, 321-326
This deals with software test management in connection with large military systems but it has much to offer to those interested in test management of smaller systems in commerce and industry. It does a good job in laying out the role of quality assurance personnel and defining the content of test plans and specifications of test procedures.

63 Myers G J, 'A Controlled Experiment in Program Testing and Code Walkthroughs/Inspections', *Communications of the ACM*, Vol. 21, No. 9, September 1978, 760-768
This describes an experiment comparing the effectiveness of black-box testing, white-box testing, and inspection methods using 59 highly experienced subjects. Performance in testing was found to be highly variable whilst inspection performance was more predictable. Performance in testing benefited when two people tested independently and pooled results. It is suggested that testing and inspection must be seen as being complementary.

64   Myers G J, *The Art of Software Testing,* (John Wiley and Sons, 1979)
      The majority in commerce and industry can learn much from this book. Some of the practices suggested might be considered impractical, eg cause-effect graphing. Others could be further developed, eg use of equivalence classes. The book contains much information of practical value and, perhaps more importantly, it considers and attempts to instill the 'right' attitude in testers.

65   Osterweil L J, 'A Strategy for Integrating Program Testing and Analysis', *Computer Program Testing,* B Chandrasekaran and S Radicchi (Eds), (North-Holland, 1981), 187-229
      In the first part of this paper various testing and analysis techniques are described, compared and contrasted. In the second, an integrated ensemble of software tools, TOOLPACK, is described.

66   Osterweil L J, Fosdick L D and Taylor R N, 'Error and Anomaly Diagnosis through Data Flow Analysis', *Computer Program Testing,* B Chandrasekaran and S Radicchi (Eds), (North-Holland, 1981), 35-63
      This is not aimed at practitioners. It goes into considerable detail of directed graph theory and requires knowledge of set theory and the notation of regular expressions.

67   Ottenstein L M, 'Quantitative Estimates of Debugging Requirements', *IEEE Transactions on Software Engineering,* Vol. SE-5, No. 5, September 1979, 504-514
      This paper suggests a basis for estimating the number of bugs in software, the computer time required for validation, and the average time to detect a bug. The method involves statistical projection and relies on many assumptions whose truth may be incomplete or imperfect. A competent mathematician could perhaps comment on the quality of the mathematics involved: the layman might be suspicious. For non-practising mathematicians, this paper will prove difficult to read.

68   Panzl D J, 'Automatic Software Test Drivers', *Computer,* Vol. 11, No. 4, April 1978, 44-50
      This is to some extent a 'selling' article extolling the virtues of General Electric's TPL2.0 test harness and demonstrating

the vices of IBM's AUT. AUT executes object code whilst
TPL2.0 'executes' source code. The article points out some
problems of both approaches. On the whole, it is fair.

69   Panzl D J, 'Automatic Revision of Formal Test Procedures',
      *Proceedings 3rd International Conference on Software
      Engineering*, 10-12 May 1978, Atlanta, Georgia, 320-326
      This article describes the use of General Electric's TPL2.0 test
      harness in reasonable detail.

70   Panzl D J, 'A Language for Specifying Software Tests', *AFIPS
      Conference Proceedings — National Computer Conference 1978*,
      5-8 June 1978, Anaheim, California, 609-619
      This describes in some detail the facilities offered by General
      Electric's TPL/F automatic test driver. TPL/F stands for Test
      Procedure Language/Fortran. The paper concludes by extolling
      the virtues of automatic test drivers.

71   Ploederer E, 'Pragmatic Techniques for Program Analysis and
      Verification', *Proceedings 4th International Conference on
      Software Engineering*, 17-19 September 1979, Munich, Germany
      This article is of interest to those with the desire and expertise
      to build a symbolic evaluator. Other computer scientists may
      find it intelligible. Non-graduates will not.

72   Polak W, 'An Exercise in Automatic Program Verification', *IEEE
      Transactions on Software Engineering*, Vol. SE-5,
      No. 5, September 1979
      This paper will probably be incomprehensible to most people:
      it requires an expert and working knowledge of verification
      by the use of logic and invariant assertions.

73   Popkin G S and Shooman M L, *On the Number of Tests
      Necessary to Verify a Computer Program*, NTIS Report RADC-
      TR-78-229 (1978)
      This sixty-page report does describe methods for determining
      the upper and lower bounds on the number of test cases
      required. Unfortunately, the methods require some matrix
      handling and zero-one integer linear programming so can only
      sensibly be used if automated. The report is interesting to the
      technically minded because it shows *how* the complexity of
      a piece of software is related to its structure.

74   Rapps S and Weyuker E J, 'Data Flow Analysis Techniques For Test Data Selection', *Proceedings 6th International Conference on Software Engineering*, 13-16 September 1982, Tokyo, Japan, 272-278
      This paper proposes a set of test aims or metrics based on data flow analysis. Unfortunately in much of the paper a formal notation is used which may cause difficulty for some readers. It is a good paper, superbly written.

75   Richardson D J and Clarke L A, 'A Partition Analysis Method to Increase Program Reliability', *Proceedings 5th International Conference on Software Engineering*, 9-12 March 1981, San Diego, California, 244-253
      Some knowledge of domains is necessary for the reader of this paper. The basic concepts reflected in it are interesting. The methodology outlined shows promise. But the claims made concerning the effectiveness of partition analysis and testing may be overstated.

76   Roman G, 'Verification Procedures Supporting Software Systems Development', *AFIPS Conference Proceedings − National Computer Conference 1979*, 4-7 June 1979, New York, 947-956
      This describes an approach to verification in the early stages of the system life cycle. The approach is used by Monsanto in St Louis. It includes semi-formal verification of a functional model of the system. Examples of these functional models are included in the paper which will be of interest to those concerned with quality assurance in a broad sense.

77   Sorkowitz A R, 'Certification Testing: A Procedure to Improve the Quality of Software Testing', *Computer*, Vol. 12, No. 8, August 1979, 20-24
      This describes the procedures and experience of the Department of Housing and Urban Development, Office of ADP Systems Development (US). Programmers, equipped only with their skill and experience, test programs then pass them to a quality assurance team. The QA team instrument the program and repeat the tests using the same test data. If the tests fail to adequately cover the program code, the program is returned to the programmer for further testing. Only 31% of programs pass at the first attempt.

78   Stucki L G, 'Automatic Generation of Self-Metric Software',
      Proceedings IEEE Symposium on Software Reliability, 1973,
      94-100
      This is primarily concerned with a software package: the
      Program Evaluator and Tester (PET). PET instruments
      programs in order to produce statistics concerning execution:
      it facilitates the measurement of test coverage. The article is
      well-illustrated with sample outputs and with statistics. PET
      instruments only Fortran programs.

79   Stucki L G, 'Software Development Tools — Acquisition
      Considerations — A Position Paper', *AFIPS Conference
      Proceedings — National Computer Conference 1977,* 13-16 June
      1977, 267-268
      The meat of this two-page paper is a one-page table providing
      superficial details of 10 software products — testing tools. It
      was useful in 1977 but is of no current value.

80   Stucki L G, 'New Directions in Automated Tools for Improving
      Software Quality', *Current Trends in Programming Methodology,*
      (Prentice-Hall, 1977), 80-111
      This article concerns itself with the 'Program Evaluator and
      Tester' system, concentrating on use of the system. The article
      is thorough and understandable.

81   Thayer T A, Lipow M and Nelson E C, *Software Reliability,*
      (North-Holland, 1978)
      Although concerned with reliability this book contains much
      of relevance to general testing. It is not however the most
      readable book: Tchebycheff inequalities, the Bayesian and
      Neyman approaches, and hyperplanes in n-dimensional space
      are all mentioned.

82   Walsh D A, 'Structured Testing', *Datamation*, July 1977, 111-118
      This describes the principles and practice of structured testing:
      path-oriented testing with a progressive strategy. It is
      considerably richer in details than most practical articles and
      is one of the few articles to consider documentation.

83   Weyuker E J and Ostrand T J, 'Theories of Program Testing
      and the Application of Revealing Subdomains', *IEEE
      Transactions on Software Engineering*, Vol. SE-6, No. 3, May

1980, 236-246
The start of this article is concerned with developing Goodenough and Gerhart's theory of test case construction. The development leads on to the theory and practice of partition analysis.

84   Weyuker E J, 'On Testing Non-testable Programs', *The Computer Journal*, Vol. 25, No. 4, 1982, 465-470
The central part of this paper deals with proving the correctness of mathematical software and may not be easy for some to follow. The remainder should however be of general interest: it is in essence a convincing argument that verifying the output of tests is as important and difficult as producing a test set.

85   White L J, 'Basic Mathematical Definitions and Results in Testing', *Computer Program Testing*, B Chandrasekaran and S Radicchi (Eds), (North-Holland, 1981), 13-24
This introduces some concepts well, eg directed graphs. It does however include considerable theory which may be difficult for the novice to follow. A working knowledge of mathematical logic is an asset for the reader.

86   White L J and Cohen E I, 'A Domain Strategy for Computer Program Testing', *IEEE Transactions on Software Engineering*, Vol. SE-6, No. 3, May 1980, 247-257
This is highly theoretical, involving the use of hyperplanes in n-dimensional space. Some useful knowledge could be gained by the mathematically knowledgeable but most people will find the paper incomprehensible.

87   White L J, Cohen E I and Zeil S J, 'A Domain Strategy for Computer Program Testing', *Computer Program Testing*, B Chandrasekaran and S Radicchi (Eds), (North-Holland, 1981), 103-113
This is essentially an abridged version of the paper included as reference 86.

88   Woodward M R, Hedley D and Hennell M A, 'Experience with Path Analysis and Testing of Programs', *IEEE Transactions on Software Engineering*, Vol. SE-6, No. 3, May 1980, 278-286
This suggests a path testing strategy based on an unconventional view of paths: paths are thought of not as sequences of decision-

decision path segments but as sequences of code blocks, each capable of uninterrupted execution and each appearing without interruption in source code. A hierarchy of coverage measures for use in such a strategy is proposed. The problem of infeasible paths is well-considered. The method involved is now known as LCSAJ testing.

89 Yourdon E, *Structured Walkthroughs,* (Yourdon Inc, 1977)
    This is thorough and readable.

90 Zeil S J and White L J, 'Sufficient Test Sets for Path Analysis Testing Strategies', *Proceedings 5th International Conference on Software Engineering,* San Diego, California, 9-12 March 1981, 184-191
    Danger — mathematicians at work!

91 Zweben S H, 'Computer Program Testing — An Introduction', *Computer Program Testing,* B Chandrasekaran and S Radicchi (Eds), (North-Holland, 1981), 3-12
    Well-written and faithful to its title.

Appendix 2
Domain Testing –
a Worked Example

In order to convey the basic principles of domain testing, it is necessary to oversimplify its use.

A sample program is shown in Figure A2.1. The program inputs only two variables I and J. The scope of the program, in terms of data, could be drawn as a rectangle on a graph which shows the value of I on one axis, the value of J on the other. This rectangle represents the program's input space. Its size is determined by the maximum and minimum acceptable values of I and J. In the illustration (Figure A2.2), it is assumed that I will be in the range −8 to +8 and J will be in the range −5 to +5.

The first job in domain testing is to partition the input space: ie to determine, in effect, the path domains within the input space. The bare rectangle already drawn implies that all combinations of I and J are treated identically. In practice, they are not: the conditional statements in the program see to that.

Consider the first conditional statement. Consider the case where I *equals* J+1 and plot a line in the rectangle to represent this case.

Statement Number	READ I,J;
1	IF I < or = J+1
2	THEN K = I+J–1;
3	ELSE K = 2*I+1;
4	IF K > or = I+1
5	THEN L = I+1;
6	ELSE L = J–1;
7	IF I = 5
8	THEN M = 2*L–K;
9	ELSE M = L+2*K–1;
	WRITE M

Figure A2.1   A Sample Program

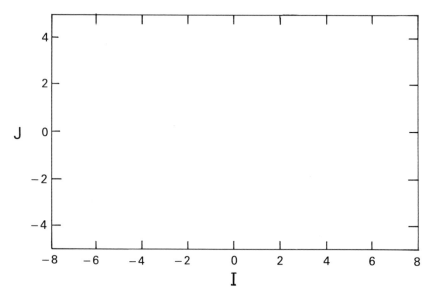

Figure A2.2   The Input Space of the Sample Program

Arrows are drawn to show that combinations of I and J occuring on the line are treated in the same way as those occuring to the left of the line. The diagram will then look like Figure A2.3.

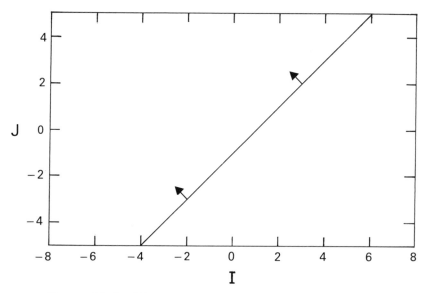

Figure A2.3   The Input Space when First Partitioned

What this diagram now shows is that so far as the operation of the program is concerned, all of the data which can be processed can be subdivided into two classes. All combinations of I and J which follow one path from the first conditional expression appear on or to the left of the diagonal. All combinations which follow the alternative path appear to the right of the diagonal.

Consider the second conditional statement. The operation of this statement depends on K. By analysing the actions of the program along the two paths between the first and second conditional expressions, it is possible to restate the second conditional expression in terms of I and J so that its operation may be represented on the graph.

Because K is calculated differently along the two paths between the first and second conditional expressions, the equation solving process must be carried out twice; once for each path. If I had been less than J+1 when the first conditional was executed, K would be equal to 2*I+1 when this second conditional statement was reached. Statement 4, the second conditional, would then be saying: IF (2*I+1) > or = (I+1). Obviously these two expressions can only be equal when I=0 so a vertical line can be drawn at I=0.

Only part of a line must be drawn; the part below the diagonal. This is because the line represents the solution of an equation which is only valid when the I less than J+1 path was followed: the line must only be drawn in the I less than J+1 area of the graph. The greater than case is equivalent to the equals case so arrows are drawn to the right to show this. The diagram then looks like Figure A2.4.

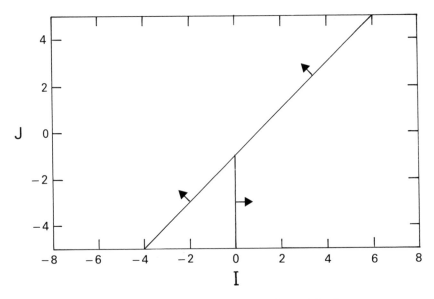

Figure A2.4   The Second Stage of Partitioning

If I had been greater than J+1 at the start of the program, by the time the second conditional was reached K would be equal to I+J−1.

Statement 4 would then effectively be saying: IF I+J−1 > or = I+1. The 'graph' representing the equals case is a horizontal line at J=2. Only part of a line must be drawn; that which is contained in the I greater than J+1 part of the graph. Arrows are drawn to show the 'greater than' case and 'equals' case are equivalent. The diagram then looks like Figure A2.5.

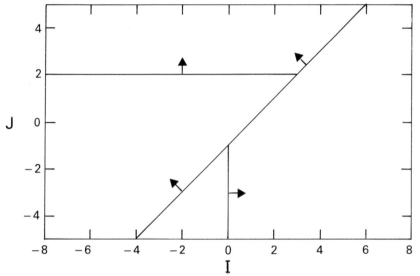

Figure A2.5   The Input Space Partitioned with Respect to Two Conditional Expressions

The third conditional statement is easy to represent because its operation is independent of the rest of the program: it is represented by a vertical line I=5. The diagram then looks like Figure A2.6.

The process outlined is not a simple procedure. In the examples shown, most of the procedure involves the following of simple rules. In more complex programs, the procedure could involve complex analytical thinking beyond the capability of most testers.

Having survived this far, the reader should find the remainder of the procedure simple. It is now necessary to allocate sets of test points to each line segment: sets of *three* test points are allocated to line segments representing tests for inequality: sets of *five* test points are

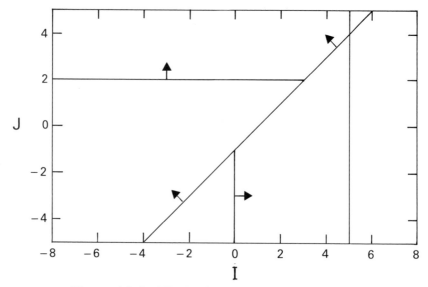

Figure A2.6   The Fully Partitioned Input Space

allocated to line segments representing tests for equality. It is of course necessary to know what is meant by the term 'line segment'. This is best demonstrated by considering the vertical line at I equals 5.

The vertical line I equals 5 represents all values of J which might occur when I equals 5 when the third conditional statement of the program is reached. This third statement may however be reached by two routes or paths.

Where J is greater than or equal to 4 one route will be followed; where J is less than 4 a second route will be followed. The upper and lower parts of the line represent the input domains of two different program paths and must therefore be tested independently. The upper and lower parts of the line must be considered as independent *line segments*. Any crossing of lines will subdivide a line into line segments. In the diagram representing the fully partitioned program, six line segments are visible: four of which relate to inequalities, two of which relate to equalities. To test the sample program for domain errors, it is necessary to plot and test no more than 22 test points (sets of test data).

In Figure A2.7, the crosses indicate the test points required to test the horizontal line segment at J equals 2 and the lower vertical line segment at I equals 5.

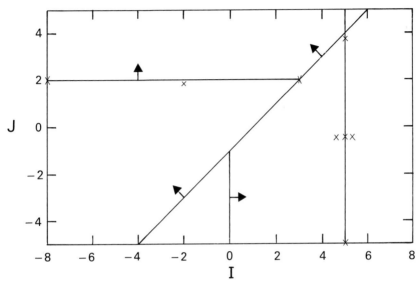

Figure A2.7   The Fully Partitioned Input Space with Two Sets of Test Points Illustrated

The horizontal line segment at J equals 2 represents an inequality and can be tested using three test points. Two are placed on the line at its extremes. The third is placed more or less centrally, off the line, but as close as possible to it on the side away from the arrows.

The value of these test points can be demonstrated by a geometric argument. If the conditional statement partially represented by the horizontal line at J equals 2 were wrong, the horizontal line at J equals 2 would not be a horizontal line at J equals 2. If the various alternative lines are considered, it becomes apparent that an error in the conditional statement would be detected.

If the correct line were higher, the two test cases *on* the line would give rise to incorrect results. If it were lower, the central point *off* the line would produce incorrect results. If it were tilted, one of the points at the ends of the line would give incorrect results.

The vertical line, below the intersection, at I=5 is tested using 5 test points. The standard configuration is as shown: three in the centre; one at each end. The value of these test points can be demonstrated by geometrical arguments similar to those already presented. It is important to note that the highest test point on this line segment is not at the extreme point − the intersection. Were it to be placed at this point it would be on the line from I=4. J=-5 to I=6, J=5 which, according to the arrows, is treated in the same way as points occuring to the left of the line. In essence, any point on this diagonal is logically above it: a test point at I=5, J=4 would be on a line segment not, at this point, being tested.

Having carried out the procedure, all that remains is to input the I and J combinations indicated by the crosses marking the test points and to verify the results produced. Because the test points are selected on the basis of what the program *does,* it is important to verify results on the basis of what the program *should do*. If any results are wrong, the program will need to be changed and the whole procedure repeated.

Appendix 3
Glossary

Action error

An action error occurs when data is processed by the right code but incorrect results are produced. Often caused by the use of incorrect literals, variables or arithmetic operands in computational and assignment statements.

Boundary error

A boundary error occurs when conditional expressions are incorrect in such a way that the boundary defining the data to be processed in a given way is then 'in the wrong place'.

Case error

A case error occurs when data which should be processed in one way is processed in some other way. A boundary error is a specific type of case error. The more general type of case error involves inverting a conditional expression so that data of type A is processed by routine B and vice versa.

Domain error

A general term to describe any error in the scope of a routine; the scope being defined in terms of the data it will process. Boundary errors and case errors are types of domain error.

Exercising

In discussing testing, the term 'exercising' is often used instead of 'executing'. It implies multiple execution with the aim of finding fault.

Missing path error

A term not used in this book. It is used to describe the omission of code.

Off-by-one error

A term not in this book. It is a specific type of boundary error which results in only one value of a data item being dealt with incorrectly. It is often caused by attempting to restate conditional expressions, eg $x < 7$ might be mistakenly coded as x not > 7.

Symbolic execution

An alternative name for symbolic evaluation.

Validation

The *active* process of proving that software has certain properties, eg correctness.

Verification

In this book, verification is used to mean the proving of a program by inductive methods. Sometimes however verificaiton is used to mean *a* process involved in proving a program. This view of verification is consistent with the view that validation is achieved by verification at numerous stages in the development life cycle.

Index